THE TRUMP PHENOMENON

How the Politics of Populism Won in 2016

SOCIETYNOW SERIES

SocietyNow: short, informed books, explaining why our world is the way it is, now.

The *SocietyNow* series provides readers with a definitive snapshot of the events, phenomena, and issues that are defining our 21st century world. Written by leading experts in their fields, and publishing as each subject is being contemplated across the globe, titles in the series offer a thoughtful, concise, and rapid response to the major political and economic events and social and cultural trends of our time.

SocietyNow makes the best of academic expertise accessible to a wider audience, to help readers untangle the complexities of each topic and make sense of our world the way it is, now.

THE TRUMP PHENOMENON

How the Politics of Populism Won in 2016

BY

PETER KIVISTO
*Augustana College and St. Petersburg
State University*

United Kingdom — North America — Japan
India — Malaysia — China

Emerald Publishing Limited
Howard House, Wagon Lane, Bingley BD16 1WA, UK

First edition 2017

Reprints and permissions service
Contact: permissions@emeraldinsight.com

British Library Cataloguing in Publication Data
A catalogue record for this book is available from the British
Library

ISBN: 978-1-78714-368-5 (Print)
ISBN: 978-1-78714-367-8 (Online)
ISBN: 978-1-78714-920-5 (Epub)

INVESTOR IN PEOPLE

Dedicated to Congressman John Lewis — who has proven his decency and courage throughout a lifetime and the memory of Ramon Casiano — who never had the chance

CONTENTS

ACKNOWLEDGMENTS

During the summer of 2016, Philippa Grand and I discussed the possibility of a short book on what we assumed would be the rise and fall of Donald Trump. The idea was to write the book in the "not-too-distant future." On November 9 we spoke again and agreed that I would begin writing at once. I did. In between these two dates, Nick Harney invited me to speak at the University of Windsor about the Trump candidacy. Even though my talk took place less than two weeks from the election, the assumption I held in August remained, though with a certain level of anxiety that was widely shared. It is to both Philippa and Nick that I owe a huge debt of gratitude for kick starting this project.

During the election season, the transition period leading up to Trump's inauguration on January 20, 2017, and the first 75 days of the administration I have had conversations and email exchanges with numerous people in the United States and Western Europe that have proved to be immensely helpful in coming to terms with what for us was both unexpected and unwelcome. Several people read all or some of the manuscript and offered their criticisms and insights, including Dag Blanck, Steve Dawdy, Thomas Faist, Kay Herrala, Susan Kivisto, Joel Phillips, and Östen Wahlbeck. Others have aided in less direct, but nevertheless much appreciated ways. This list includes academic colleagues, students, friends, and family members. At the risk of leaving out names, I want to express my gratitude to the following: Richard Alba, Jeffrey Alexander, Fathimatha Ali, Bob Antonio, Imam Saad Baig, Paolo Boccagni, Clara Caldwell (who at age 88 took part in the Woman's March in Washington, DC, on January 21, 2017, along with her daughter, granddaughter, and great granddaughter), John Caldwell, Rev. Robin Caldwell, Angie Carter, Naomi Castro, Rev. Jeffrey Clements, Paul Croll, Cheryl Erdmann, Don Erickson, Nancy Foner, Mary Hall, Lena Hann, Katie Hanson, Beth Hartung, David Hill, Carrie Hough, Ella Iacoviello, Corrie Jandourek, Shirley Johnson, Adam Kaul, Aaron Kivisto, Katie Kivisto, Sarah Kivisto, Sonja Knudsen, Auvo Kostianen, Lauren Langman, Joe McDowell, Irene Mekus, Rachel Moody, Ewa Morawska, Donald Munro, Sara Munro, Wendy Ng, Niko Pyrohönen, Andrey Rezaev, Fatima Sattar, Keila Saucedo, Pasi Saukonen, Giuseppe Sciortino, Jean Sottos, Vince Thomas, Rhys Williams, Jake Wirtala, and Kathy Wirtala.

CHAPTER 1

INTRODUCTION

On November 8, 2016, American voters elected Donald J. Trump to become the 45th President of the United States. He was a candidate who had been widely criticized, described as authoritarian in his leadership style and whose psychological fitness for office was frequently called into question, with mental health experts concluding that his behavior reveals what could be an undiagnosed personality disorder. American voters elected him despite Trump being viewed as an unusual candidate running a highly unconventional election campaign. They did so even though negative views of him have been as high as 70%, which suggests that some people who viewed him negatively nevertheless voted for him. They did so even though he was a central figure over several years in stoking the birther conspiracy theory that sought to delegitimize the election of the nation's first black President. They did so even though his bullying and name-calling of his Republican rivals was uncivil, revealing a lack of respect for those he competed against for the nomination. They did so even though his braggadocio is adolescent and incessant (claiming, e.g., that his "IQ is one of the highest" and that he has the "world's greatest memory"). They did so even though Trump demonized Mexicans as criminals, rapists, and drug dealers and suggested that the Mexican government was responsible for orchestrating their migration to the United States. They did so even though he called for a ban on all Muslims entering the country, a violation of constitutional protections of religious freedom.

They did so despite his repeated threats to send Hillary Clinton to prison, the sort of threats one expects to hear from cult-of-personality dictators, but not from a candidate vying for election in a democratic nation. They did so even though a standard part of Trump campaign rallies and in numerous tweets was to call reporters "dishonest," "scum," "slime," and "liars." They did so even though he repeated conspiracy theories and gained support from far right groups. They did so even though Trump's frequent use of his Twitter account was often viewed as revealing a lack of self-control.

They did so despite a history of misogyny, and in bragging that was caught on a hot mike that because he was a celebrity he could sexually assault women. They did so even though he was accused of mocking a reporter with a physical handicap. They did so even though he claimed Senator John McCain was not a war hero because after his plane went down during the Vietnam War, he ended up a prisoner of war. They did so despite his verbal attacks on the Khan family after Mr. Khan had spoken at the Democratic National Convention — Muslim Americans and a Gold Star family whose middle son, a commissioned officer in the US Army, was killed in Iraq. They did so even though his saber rattling has unnerved high ranking members of the military and the intelligence community. They did so despite a history of investigations and reportage on his business career that questioned Trump's own claims regarding his business acumen. They did so even though at the Republican Party convention, Trump's self-belief led him to contend that in addressing the problems confronting the nation, "I alone can fix it." They did so even though his repetitious claim that he would make America great again was never followed up with realistic policy proposals. Rather, they appeared ready to believe that he was going to spend massively on infrastructure and on building up the military while simultaneously slashing taxes and containing the deficit. Unlike the majority of adult Americans who did not vote for Trump, those who did appeared to be willing to engage in a form of magical thinking.

How was a person so many people, in public life and privately, had concluded was unfit for the office elected to lead the largest and most powerful democracy in the world? And what does it mean for that democracy? Does it mean that little will change as *Washington Post* columnist Kathleen Parker implied shortly before Election Day in a column bearing the headline, "Calm Down. We'll Be Fine No Matter Who Wins." Or does turning over the reins of power to such a person constitute a genuine test of the robustness of American democracy, or even more bleakly, an existential threat? Laying my cards on the table, I would gladly present Ms. Parker with the Dr. Pangloss Award for 2016, while concurring with conservative columnist, Michael Gerson, when he wrote in the *Washington Post* two weeks before the election that, "It is the first time in my political lifetime that I have seen fragility at the heart of American democracy."

This book is an effort to offer an account of Trump's political rise and ultimate electoral victory, and in doing so it seeks to identify some of the implications of what it might portend for the future. It will discuss events leading up to the election and beyond as the Trump operatives geared up to take over the reins of government on January 20, 2017, but it stops with the swearing in. What happens once this administration begins to govern is a topic for another day. The book at hand proceeds by first exploring who Donald Trump is, the goal of which is to sketch out three analytically distinct but nevertheless intertwined anti-Trump narratives that have emerged and acquired sufficient robustness to have a continued impact on public opinion. It includes a narrative about his psychology or temperament, one concerning his long career in business, and the third addressing his political worldview. Trump's life has been both vividly on display in the public eye as he has enthusiastically sought attention throughout his business career, but aspects of his world — particularly regarding his business holdings — are far from transparent.

Next the book looks at who supported him, seeking to discern who they were and to understand why they voted for this celebrity businessman. This gets into more complex territory, and one can assume that political analysts — journalists, social scientists, and political operatives — will be working over voting data for some time to come. Nonetheless, we do know quite a lot about his supporters and do not need to wait for the future for some basic answers. In addition, there is a large body of scholarship that has offered varied accounts of voters who have in other places and times opted for authoritarian candidates running as populists. I will frame this analysis of Trump voters considering that body of work.

Third, I look at those forces that enabled, or made possible his, in many respects, unlikely success. While not the only forces, the three most significant are the media, the Christian Right, and the Republican Party. The book concludes with an analysis of Trumpism as a manifestation of right-wing populism and will use insights from scholars who are involved in producing comparative analyses of this movement in Europe and North America at a historical moment where it has become a phenomenon of major political significance on both sides of the Atlantic.

I make no effort to present anything remotely resembling the last word on the topic. I see it rather as a preliminary reconnaissance, and am fully aware that there is already underway a veritable cottage industry of critiques of the Trump phenomenon and the fruits of such labors will begin to appear soon. My hope is simply that this slim volume will contribute to that needed conversation. More than that, this is a moment when such dialogue must be a prelude to actions devoted to defending democracy. But such actions will take place in an uncomfortable time and space. Indeed, on the last day of 2016, Donald Trump tweeted the following message: "Happy New Year to all, including my many enemies and those who have fought me and lost so badly they just don't know what to do. Love!" A colleague forwarded this message to me with the subject heading: "A crazy Trump tweet that sums up the next four years?"

The uncomfortable time and space I refer to was recently diagnosed by sociologist Neil Gross as an indication that a large swathe of the American citizenry is experiencing collective trauma, a term he sees deriving from the seminal theorizing of the early French sociologist Émile Durkheim. He contended over a century ago that when the bases of social solidarity are undermined by challenges to customary shared beliefs and practices rooted in norms, values, and ritual behaviors, people can collectively suffer from what Durkheim called anomie, but which might more familiarly be described as a feeling of alienation or disorientation. This is the feeling currently experienced by many anti-Trump Americans, according to Gross, and the reason goes well beyond the fact that the polls predicted a Clinton victory. He writes:

> For progressives, moderates, and "Never Trump"
> Republicans, the political order they long took for
> granted — defined by polarization, yes, but also by

*a commitment to basic principles of democracy and
decency — is suddenly gone. In recent decades,
Democrats and Republicans rarely agreed on
substance, but all candidates for major office were
expected to adhere to fundamental ethical norms,
like "don't threaten to jail your opponent" and
"don't celebrate sexual assault."*

*Mr. Trump's victory signals that that world, with the
assurances it offered that there were some lines those
seeking power wouldn't cross (or the American
electorate won't let them cross), is no longer. (Gross,
2016, p. 3)*

In short, for a large swath of the American population
there is an uncomfortable sense that serious damage has been
done to the body politic and to the well-being of civil society.
The following three chapters, which can be read as an effort
to offer an account of how this damage was inflicted, will
reveal that there is no simple or quick fix. The root of the
problem transcends Trump, who should be seen as a consequence rather than as a cause of a systemic failure to inocu-
late the democratic process from the clarion call of
authoritarianism.

CHAPTER 2

DEMOCRATIC CULTURE AND CIVIC VIRTUE

Consider the following propositions. First, democracy is to be preferred over authoritarianism. Second, no democracy in the past has been as democratic as it might have been. This point was underscored by President Barack Obama in his last international speech while in office. Speaking in Athens on November 16, 2016, he reflected on that city's "most precious of gifts" bequeathed to the world, the idea of democracy. At the same time, he went on to note that "the earliest forms of democracy here in Athens were far from perfect — just as the early forms of democracy in the United States were far from perfect." Third, no currently existing democracy is as democratic as it could be. Fourth, the persistence of democracy over time cannot be taken for granted. What follows is premised on these propositions, though it is the fourth one that will be its focus. Put simply, the question raised in this and the following two chapters is whether or not democracy in America — however flawed it might be — is currently threatened by a degrading of its democratic culture and with it a shared sense of bedrock civic virtues that in normal times guide the actions of both ordinary citizens and elected officials.

Democratic political systems are characterized by three key procedural patterns that set them apart from despotic alternatives and, in fact, are intended to serve as barriers to antidemocratic tendencies: institutionalized mechanisms insuring that citizens can play a role in governance, limitations placed on the power of leaders, and a commitment to the rule of law, which supersedes that of any leader or segment of the citizenry. Democracy when it works well provides governance that is both responsible and responsive to the needs of citizens and the best interests of the society at large.

Yet, in contrast to that civics class overview of democracy as an ideal, the real world is rather different. This should not be surprising insofar as politics is the arena in which competing views and interests vie with each other for power in seeking to direct public policy and governmental action in one direction or another. As an arena of contestation and conflict, typically politics plays out with an admixture of civility and incivility. When the latter gets the upper hand, we enter into the territory of what political scientist Susan Herbst calls "rude democracy." A level of incivility ought to be considered par for the course, but only if incivility does not trump civility. When it does, the culture of democracy is degraded.

That culture is nurtured in civil society, which is that "space" — sometimes a physical space, but more significantly a symbolic space — wherein, as Yale sociologist Jeffrey C. Alexander (2006) has argued, conceptualizations of social solidarity and justice take shape and are various resisted, revised, or reformulated over time. When the civil has an edge over the uncivil, solidarity is construed in an expansive and inclusive way, whereas when the uncivil has the upper hand, a more constrictive and exclusionary view of solidarity takes hold. Likewise, polar contrasts will be found in views surrounding topics associated with justice, freedom, and equality predicated on whether articulated in a civil or an uncivil frame.

In Alexander's analysis of Barack Obama's electoral victory over John McCain in 2008 and again, with Bernadette Jaworsky, in an analysis of the 2012 re-election victory over challenger Mitt Romney, considerable attention is devoted to the narratives that both sides sought to promote — narratives that both projected their respective candidates as models of civic virtue and their opponents as in key respects falling short (Alexander and Jaworsky, 2014). These narratives constitute a central part of the script in the drama of democracy, and the fate of a candidate hinges on the extent to which the citizen audience finds one narrative more convincing than the other. As Alexander observed at the outset of *The Performance of Politics*, "In the course of political campaigns, those struggling for power are subject to a terrible scrutiny. This is critical because, once power is achieved, it gains significant independence from civil society" (Alexander, 2010, p. 7).

In this regard, the evidence suggests that voting is more a matter of leadership selection than it is an issue-oriented focus in which ordinary citizens are intent on, in the words of the late political scientist Robert Dahl "determining the policies" that will come to define an understanding of the good society. It's not that issues are unimportant at election time, but rather that they play a secondary role to settling on a preferred candidate worthy of one's vote. In making their decisions, voters are not atomistic individuals, but rather are grounded in various social identities, some of which are more salient than others. Insofar as this is the case, people's political choices are made on the basis of what political scientists Christopher H. Achen and Larry M. Bartels call their "partisan hearts and spleens." Social identities provide people with political predispositions that make them more or less amenable to the appeal of contrasting campaign narratives.

Narratives are socially constructed. As such, they are not the product of any one individual, but rather take shape as an interactional outcome of numerous voices. Those voices originate among those sectors of the population most engaged with politics: journalists, editorial writers, and other voices in the media, various experts and intellectuals, and people who make a living off of politics. The purpose of narratives is to persuade the large majority of the citizenry that pays scant attention to politics until election season to either support or oppose a candidate. Thus, as Table 2.1 indicates,

Table 2.1. Civil versus Uncivil Leadership Traits.

Civil Virtues	Uncivil Vices
Responsible	Irresponsible
Knowledgeable	Ill-informed
Reasonable	Irrational
Even-tempered	Vengeful
Self-disciplined	Erratic
Respectful	Disrespectful
Law-abiding	Corrupt
Honest	Dishonest
Motivated by a commitment to public service	Motivated by self-interest
Respect for the rule of law	Contempt for the rule of law
Calm	Excitable
Prudent	Rash
Articulate	Inarticulate

narratives are constructed by depicting as binaries various civil virtues versus uncivil vices: responsible versus irresponsible, knowledgeable versus ill-informed, reasonable versus irrational, and so on. What distinguished the 2016 campaign from previous ones was that the winner of the election had been the subject of not one, but three negative narratives. Furthermore, the narratives' creators could be located on both the political center-left and center-right, part of what historian Arthur Schlesinger, Jr. at the dawn of the Cold War called the "vital center" essential to protecting an imperfect democracy from the temptations of authoritarianism. It is that vital center that today, in the view of Yale sociologist Philip Gorski, "is threatened by a new set of centrifugal forces." He stresses that what he means by the vital center is decidedly not a "mushy middle that splits the differences between the Left and the Right." Nor is it Third Way that makes irrelevant the Left-Right divide. Rather it is seen as a "political vocabulary that enables dialogue and debate between Left and Right," the purpose of which is "not to end debate but to restart it" (Gorski, 2017, pp. 1–2).

One can read the three narratives that will be described in this chapter as emanating from the voices of individuals located in the vital center. Despite their political differences and backgrounds, the particular accounts they present reflect a shared perspective on the Trump candidacy as antithetical to the healthy functioning of a liberal democracy. Of course during the campaign positive narratives also developed that were wholly supportive of Trump, and many commentators and Trump supporters questioned the negative narratives outlined in this chapter. Supporters viewed Trump as a successful businessman, a take-charge guy, someone who understood and spoke for "the forgotten" men and women of America — and it was that view, those narratives, that, of course, won out in the end. But what follows specifically sets out to examine the "narratives of opposition" that evolved around Trump the candidate, and became the dominant narrative of the mainstream media, leading many to believe he could not and would not win, setting into context the discussion that follows on why he was able to win. How was someone so vilified by so many able to gain the highest office?

Who is Donald Trump and how did many arrive at a particular consensus about him? In answering the first question, the short answer is this. Trump was born on June 14, 1946, one of five children born to Fred and Mary (née MacLeod). Trump's paternal grandfather was a German immigrant whose lucrative business ventures staked his son Fred, who in turn bequeathed — estimates vary considerably in the complicated world of Trump businesses — between $40 million and $200 million to his son. Trump's brashness and quest for celebrity status provided him with widespread name recognition. Because his main business ventures were initially rooted in New York City, he would not necessarily have become a recognizable figure at the national level. However, his ability to gain notoriety about his personal life in the tabloid press and his willingness to be a frequent guest on such programs as Howard Stern's shock jock radio show helped considerably to make his name familiar across the country. Likewise, his widely touted book, *The Art of the Deal*, first published in 1987, served to promote him as a successful businessman whose insights could be profitably employed by would-be entrepreneurs. But perhaps the most important vehicle for gaining national name recognition was his role as host of *The Apprentice*, a reality television program that first aired in 2004.

Despite this very high profile role in the spotlight, the reality is that Trump was not well known — or at least he wasn't until his announcement to run for the Presidency on June 16, 2015. One reason for this lack of familiarity was, quite simply, that the media didn't take his candidacy seriously and their general impression of him as a modern P. T. Barnum meant that his entry was seen purely for its entertainment value. The assumption was widely held that he would eventually either drop out of the race or implode. Thus, it was not worth the time or energy to seek out the "real" Trump, though over the years journalists had presented plenty of material about his personality and the way he conducted his business operations. Once he became the Republican nominee, efforts to better understand who he is moved into high gear. What has emerged is a portrait of an individual that has led to global concerns about what the prospect of a Trump administration means for the future of the world's largest democracy. The composite portraits that follow are based on numerous accounts that have been divided into three distinct narratives: Trump's psychological make-up or character, his career as a businessman, and assessments that his political worldview reflects authoritarian tendencies.

CHARACTER

Late in the summer of 2016, as the Presidential campaign was moving into overdrive, the headline of Pulitzer prize winning syndicated columnist Eugene Robinson's August first column in *The Washington Post* was "Is Donald Trump Just Plain Crazy?" In answering his own question, Robinson wrote that though earlier he may have thought that Trump was "being crazy like a fox" he had become convinced that "he's just plain crazy," going on to write that "it would be irresponsible to ignore the fact that Trump's grasp on reality appears to be tenuous at best." To amplify his claim, he made three observations and offered examples to back them up: (1) "he lies the way other people breathe"; (2) "he's alarmingly thin-skinned"; and (3) "Trump is the worst kind of bully."

On the same day, a column by Robert Kagan, a neo-conservative commentator and fellow at the Brookings Institution, appeared in the same newspaper, in this case its headline stating, "There Is Something Very Wrong with Donald Trump." Kagan contended that Trump is "a man with a disordered personality," leaving "it to the professionals to determine exactly what to call it." His bill of particulars focused on Trump's lack of empathy, his need to strike out against any and all perceived slights, and his lack of self-control. Kagan argued that his challenges to political correctness are often racist or misogynistic, but at other times they are "just childish: making fun of someone's height, or suggesting that someone's father was involved in the Kennedy assassination." Kagan concluded that Trump's unnamed "psychological pathologies are ultimately self-destructive."

Three days later in the same publication, conservative columnist and (non-practicing) psychiatrist Charles Krauthammer entered the discussion about Trump's psychological unfitness for the Presidency, writing that his

> *hypersensitivity and unedited, untampered*
> *Pavlovian responses are, shall we say, unusual in*
> *both ferocity and predictability. This is beyond nar-*
> *cissism. I used to think Trump was an 11-year old,*
> *an undeveloped schoolyard bully. I was off by about*
> *10 years. His needs are more primitive, an infantile*
> *hunger for approval and praise, a craving that can*
> *never be satisfied. He lives in a cocoon of solipsism*
> *where the world outside himself has value — indeed*
> *exists — only insofar as it sustains and inflates him.*

And finally, *New York Times* op-ed writer David Brooks, writing in December 2016, offered a precise diagnosis by contending that Trump is afflicted with narcissistic alexithymia, which he defines as

> *the inability to understand or describe the emotions in the self. Unable to know themselves, sufferers are unable to understand, relate, or attach to others. To prove their own existence, they hunger for endless attention from the outside. Lacking internal measures of their own worth, they rely on external but insecure criteria like wealth, beauty, fame, and others' submission.*

Brooks went on to characterize Trump's relationships with women as one in which "he can only hate and demean them" and as a person who in general can relate to others only by bullying and insulting and whose emotional register revolves around expressions of "fury and aggression." No doubt, the incident that penetrated into the public psyche most vividly in this connection was the "Access Hollywood" tape from 2005 in which Trump asserted that his celebrity status permitted him to "grab 'em [women] by the pussy." When several women subsequently came forward charging Trump with assault or attempted assault, which he himself denied, he threatened to sue them.

The narcissistic label had been the one most commonly used by critics trying to make sense of Trump's character. In the age of the *Diagnostic and Statistical Manual (DSM-V)*, used by clinicians, researchers, the pharmaceutical industry, and insurance companies to classify mental disorders, many have turned to this reference book to see how it describes narcissistic personality disorder. The manual lists nine items under this personality disorder: (1) exhibits a grandiose sense of self-importance; (2) expresses fantasies of unlimited success, power, brilliance, and beauty; (3) sees oneself as special and unique; (4) requires excessive admiration; (5) has a sense of entitlement; (6) is interpersonally exploitative; (7) lacks empathy; (8) is envious of others; and (9) is arrogant and haughty.

It should be noted that there are critics of such attempts to offer assessments of the psychological state of political candidates, and there has been an ongoing debate among psychiatrists and psychologists on the ethics of diagnosing Trump from a distance. The efforts of scholars to engage in "psycho-historical inquiry," the term the late historian, Bruce Mazlish, used to describe his attempt to understand the conflicting inner forces shaping the mind of Richard Nixon, have met considerable resistance. More relevant here is the aftermath of a survey of psychiatrists about the psychological fitness of Barry Goldwater during his run for the Presidency in 1964. Though the survey had a very low response rate, a majority of those who responded assessed Goldwater as unfit for the role. Goldwater sued the magazine and won, and in response the American Psychiatric Association passed what became known as the Goldwater Rule, which as part of the psychiatric code of ethics required psychiatrists to refrain from diagnosing individuals they had not seen in therapeutic settings. This rule does not prevent nonpsychiatrists from offering, based on the evidence at hand, their own good-faith assessments of the psychological character of political candidates, doing so with the conviction that advancing the public good requires asking such questions.

And, in fact, within the psychiatric community there are voices such as those of Jerome Kroll and Claire Pouncey arguing that psychiatrists as citizens who happen to have specialized knowledge have not simply a right but an obligation to provide insights into the character of candidates for high office (Koerth-Baker, 2016). Numerous other mental-health professionals have echoed this and have publicly described Trump as narcissistic, including Harvard developmental psychologist Howard Gardner, and clinical psychologists George Simon and Ben Michaelis, the latter noting that, "He's so classic that I'm archiving video clips of him because there is no better example [of narcissistic personality disorder]" (Alford, 2015).

Taking a somewhat different but parallel approach, Northwestern University clinical psychologist Dan P. McAdams, in a long essay in *The Atlantic*, refrained from discussing narcissistic personality order and instead focused on what he calls the Big Five personality dimensions: extroversion, neuroticism, conscientiousness, agreeableness, and openness. An individual's personality is defined in terms of where they are located on a continuum for each of these dimensions. Most people score somewhere in the middle on all five dimensions, and personality traits tend to remain stable across a lifetime. McAdams noted at the outset that given how well documented Trump's life history has been, the behavioral evidence is there to draw conclusions.

He began by stating that, "Trump's personality is certainly extreme by any standard, and particularly rare for a presidential candidate." Specifically, his profile reveals "sky-high extroversion combined with off-the-chart low agreeableness," a conclusion McAdam sees as widely held by Trump observers. High extroversion leads the individual to "relentless reward-seeking. Prompted by dopamine circuits in the brain, highly extroverted actors are driven to pursue positive emotional experiences, whether they come in the form of social approval, fame, or wealth." While Trump's exaggerated level of extroversion may be extreme, McAdams's thinks that his low level of agreeableness is even more extreme, a trait seen throughout his life — expressed by being "callous, rude, arrogant, and lacking empathy." This is linked to McAdam's assessment that "the emotional core around which Donald Trump's personality constellates is anger," which permeates his humor and his political rhetoric.

Trump is described in these narratives as operating with a dichotomous worldview that divides everybody into two categories: those he defines as "losers" or as "disgusting" versus those who are "great." The word "disgusting" comes up frequently when Trump speaks, McAdams suggesting that this word choice may reflect Trump's self-acknowledged germaphobia. Disgusting people are those who have in some way challenged or criticized him, while the latter are those who he perceives to be on his side or people who are, at least for the moment, useful to him. This dichotomous worldview is further seen as contributing to his oft-commented on limited vocabulary, which manifests itself in the formulaic nature of his condemnations and expressions of approval (McAdams, 2016).

Such conclusions about Trump's personality traits are based largely on observations of his public presentations of self, which has led some to ponder whether there is a different private life. In an interview conducted for *The New Yorker* in the late 1990s after Trump's divorce to first wife Ivana, Mark Singer observed the public Trump and in various ways tried to get Trump to talk about himself when alone. The questions appeared to perplex Trump, and in a final attempt to get him to reveal something about his inner self, Singer asked if he considered himself to be "ideal company." Trump replied, "You really want to know what I consider ideal company? A total piece of ass." Singer concluded his article with the following damning assessment: Trump, he wrote, "had aspired to and achieved the ultimate luxury, an existence unmolested by the rumbling of a soul." (Trump himself was not happy with the article, which later appeared in a collection by Singer entitled *Character Studies: Encounters with the Curiously Obsessed*, published in 2005. In a letter to the *New York Times* Trump wrote that Singer "was not born with great writing ability" and noted that "some people cast shadows and other people choose to live in those shadows.")

The idea that Trump's public persona is one with his private persona was further endorsed by Tony Schwartz, ghostwriter of Trump's book *The Art of the Deal*, who contended that "there is no private Trump." Despite having written a highly unflattering and critical account of Trump as a swaggering bully who tried and failed to evict tenants in rent-controlled and stabilized units in a Central Park South building he had purchased, he was hired by Trump to write his book of business advice. Schwartz realized retrospectively that what he saw as a take-down of Trump was perceived at that moment by Trump as positive public relations given that he wanted to establish himself in the public's mind as a tough, hard-charging entrepreneur. Ironically, Schwartz claims that when he asked for half of the half-million-dollar advance and half of royalties, Trump agreed without negotiating the deal, landing the author a percentage of the take far exceeding what is typical for ghostwriters (Mayer 2016a).

Over a period of 18 months, Schwartz believes he learned a considerable amount about the man. He took detailed notes and kept a journal, but because he then saw himself to be implicated in creating an image of Trump that wasn't based on the reality he had witnessed, and because he had profited handsomely from what he saw as hack work, he kept quiet over the years. But when Trump became a contender for the Republican Party's nomination for President, the fact that he had "put lipstick on a pig" led him to feel "deep remorse." Thus, he came forward and told his story in a July 2016 *New Yorker* profile by Jane Mayer. In summary, his account offers the following portrait. Trump, he discovered, was "pathologically impulsive and self-centered." Schwartz reinforced the conclusion that Trump divides the world into two camps, that of the "scummy loser, liar" and that of "the greatest," the really "world-class."

The most revealing aspect of Trump's psyche not quite captured by others but apparently immediately evident to Schwartz was that Trump "has no attention span." Though Schwartz does not offer a diagnosis, he does draw the conclusion that Trump exhibits "a stunning level of superficial knowledge and just plain ignorance." Schwartz suspects that Trump has never read an entire book in his adult life, never seeing a book anywhere in his office or apartment. Mayer notes that other reporters have suspected that Trump is not a reader, and when Fox News journalist Megyn Kelly asked him in an interview to talk about any book he had recently read, he admitted as much, contending "I don't have the time." Mayer contrasts his anti-intellectualism not only to the professorial Barack Obama, but also to George W. Bush, a person often criticized as a lightweight but who engaged in a friendly reading competition with his advisor Karl Rove.

Based in particular on Schwartz's listening in on Trump business calls, which Trump approved, the writer concluded that, "Lying is second nature to him. More than anyone else I have ever met, Trump has the ability to convince himself that whatever he is saying at any given moment is true, or sort of true, or at least *ought* to be true." He went on to state that, "He lied strategically. He had a complete lack of conscience about it" noting perceptively that since most of us are "constrained by the truth" Trump's lack of a similar control "gave him a strange advantage" in dealing with others.

Schwartz in what he says is his lasting regret offered what he now describes as a deceptive spin by calling Trump's lies "truthful hyperbole." Whereas Trump loved the term, Schwartz sees deceit for what it is, which is never "innocent."

In *The Art of the Deal* Schwartz puts the following words into his fictional Trump: "I don't do if for the money. I've got enough, much more than I'll ever need. I do it to do it. Deals are my art form." In his interview with Mayer, Schwartz says that, "He would be incapable of saying something like that — it wouldn't even be in his vocabulary."

Trump did contest Schwartz's analysis of him. In July 2016, *The New Yorker* reprinted a cease-and-desist letter to Schwartz from the Trump Organization, issued in response to Mayer's article, asserting that Schwartz had made defamatory statements, and concluding "your statements are not only completely disingenuous but replete with outright lies, false and destructive statements and downright fabrications which you fully know to be untrue (Mayer 2016b)."

Trump's personality came under intense scrutiny during the election campaign, with critical commentators establishing a narrative that questioned his fitness for office and demonstrated uncivil vices that run counter to the virtues required of democratic leadership. In particular, they depicted him as being irresponsible, vengeful, disrespectful, dishonest, and motivated by self-interest. The composite portrait created by these multiple attempts to make sense of Donald Trump's character lead critics to the conclusion that it can be understood in terms of three drives: for money, attention, and revenge. Those commentators contend that he has exhibited an inability to feel empathy, which they link to his red-in-tooth-and-claw view of the world, which he depicts as one of constant struggle to survive, a struggle that forces him to strike out harshly against anyone perceived to be in the way. Their shared view is summed up in journalist Michael D'Antonio's report in his 2016 book *The Truth About Trump* that Trump told him in an interview that "[for] the most part, you can't respect people because most people aren't worthy of respect."

BUSINESS CAREER

While the preceding narrative concerning Trump's inner life is of relatively recent vintage, the anti-Trump narrative concerning his business career has developed over an extended period of time. This should not be surprising given that Trump has been a businessman in New York City for decades and has actively courted media attention throughout his entire career. Readers will be familiar with this narrative insofar as it was part of the rhetoric employed by Hillary Clinton and her campaign surrogates, and elicited considerable media attention. Thus, rather than offering summary accounts of what amounts to a remarkably thick collective narrative description, I would simply suggest that those who want to immerse themselves in the details consult books by Gwenda Blair (who had remarkable access to Trump when she began researching his family's background in the 1980s), Michael D'Antonio (2016), David Cay Johnston (2016), Timothy O'Brien (2005), and *The Washington Post* team of Michael Kranish and Marc Fisher (2016). The conclusions of these books offer mutually reinforcing negative portraits, which have been further reinforced by other business journalists working for several mainstream newspapers and magazines [see for example Austen (2016); Cassidy (2016); Craig (2016); Eaglesham, Maremont, & Schwartz (2016); Eichenwald (2016); Fahrenthold (2016a); Farhi (2016); Helderman (2016); Martin (2016); Rosenthal (2016); Stuart (2016)].

The anti-Trump narrative challenges his campaign's portrayal of him as a successful businessman with the negotiating skills needed to create a business empire. This characterization was attractive to a right-wing worldview that, in the words of University of Michigan sociologist Margaret Somers, engages in "romancing the market" while "reviling the state." This perspective has been prominent in such circles since Ronald Reagan's assertion that government was part of the problem not part of the solution, which has fueled an unquestioned — but empirically unsubstantiated — belief that businesspersons can readily translate the values and behaviors of the economic sphere to the political, and indeed should do so. The essence of neoliberalism, such a conviction seeks to replace the dialogical decision-making necessary for the functioning of a pluralist liberal democracy with the autocratic top-down decision-making of the modern corporation.

The anti-Trump narrative challenge has pointed to a career that has included a major federal lawsuit involving racial discrimination in rental policy, a legacy of lawsuits and counter-lawsuits, and highlighted business failures resulting in multiple bankruptcies. It has pointed to his involvement with business associates with questionable legal histories, while arguing that the Trump Organization is structured in a way that precludes transparency. It has questioned why Trump would become involved in activities such as Trump University, which was taken to court for fraud and ultimately agreed to pay a settlement of $25 million. It has also questioned Trump's claim to be a major contributor to various philanthropies. And finally, it has countered the widespread impression that Trump is a major figure in the American business world. Here the sober and succinct assessment appearing in *The Economist* (2016) depicts the Trump organization as "a small, middle-aged and largely domestic property business," going on to write that "If the Trump family members are to make a second fortune in the next four years, they will have to reinvent a mediocre firm." The article locates the Trump Organization as the 833rd largest firm in the United States by market value and 1925th by sales.

POLITICAL WORLDVIEW

Unlike the detailed chronological narrative that has developed over time addressing Trump's business career, the narrative about his political worldview has largely taken shape during the past year. Earlier understandings of his political orientation tended to view him as a pliable operator with few if any deeply held convictions — either a pragmatist or someone potentially easily manipulated. He sought power, but toward what ends was uncertain. However, as his campaign gained momentum, opinion makers and political analysts began to create a different narrative, one that focused on Trump's presumed authoritarianism and as this perspective took shape, so too did a discourse arguing that his candidacy constituted a threat to liberal democracy. As part of this discourse, and in stark contrast to any election campaign in modern history, the term "fascism" entered into the conversation.

In trying to get at the essence of fascism, Umberto Eco reflected on his own experience of growing up in Mussolini's Italy, the locus of what he considers to be "ur-fascism." Less an ideology, he writes, it is far more a matter of specific ways of thinking and feeling, derived from cultural sensibilities that were in turn shaped by "obscure instincts and unfathomable drives," the net result of which is the promotion of "a *fuzzy* totalitarianism." Much would be written about totalitarianism in the aftermath of World War II, but until recently, totalitarianism has receded as a category of analysis in what was too optimistically seen as a post-communist, post-fascist world. While the former is not making a comeback, the latter is, certainly in many European nations. But what about the United States? What can be said in responding to this question is that Donald Trump is the first presidential candidate of a major political party in the history of the nation to raise the following question from serious mainstream political commentators — from the center-right as well as the center-left: Is Donald Trump a fascist?

To cite two examples of opinion writers from across the political spectrum who have answered the question affirmatively, neoconservative Robert Kagan, referred to earlier in this chapter, contends that Trump's candidacy, which he considered to be a "singular threat to our democracy" is predicated not on actual policy proposals or a coherent ideology, but rather on "an attitude, an aura of crude strength, and machismo, a boasting disrespect for the niceties of ... democratic culture." Kagan observes that the fascist movements of the middle of the twentieth century were likewise a bundle of contradictions, offering a strongman in place of a genuine political agenda. He claims that what is distinctive about the Trump phenomenon is that in America fascism comes, "not with jackboots and salutes (although there have been salutes, and a whiff of violence) but with a television huckster, a phony billionaire, a textbook egomaniac 'tapping into' popular resentments and insecurities, and with an entire national party — out of ambition or political loyalty, or simply out of fear — falling into line behind him" (Kagan, 2016b).

Liberal commentator Robert Reich, former Secretary of Labor in the Clinton administration and a professor at Berkeley, concurs with Kagan that fascism replaces policy and rational arguments in a democratic forum by offering a strongman "whose personal power would remedy all ills." Reich notes that twentieth century fascists created cults of personality, relied on intimidating and threatening opponents, encouraged violence, promoted ideas of national strength by vilifying enemies usually described in xenophobic ways, and ignored international law. Contending that Trump fits the pattern of these fascists from the past in each of these items, he concludes that it is for this reason that "Donald Trump presents such a profound danger to the future of

America and the world." This view is echoed in the full-page advertisement in the *New York Times* that appeared on page A7 of the January 4, 2017 edition paid for by a new organization called Refuse Fascism. The signatories contended that, "By any definition, Donald Trump is a fascist," going on to state that, "Fascism foments and relies on xenophobic nationalism, racism, misogyny, and the aggressive re-institution of oppressive 'traditional values'."

Other critical commentators, seeking to use an understanding of the term fascism in a more historically contextualized and delimited manner, are less inclined to see such a clear and present danger — regardless of whether Trump the person represents a manifestation of ur-fascism. Instead, as Sarah Grey concludes, he ought to be seen as a precursor to fascism. She quotes Robert Paxton as defining fascism as being in part "a form of political behavior marked by obsessive preoccupation with community decline, humiliation or victimhood." This fits with Trump's campaign message about how low America had fallen and how he alone could restore it to its lost greatness. His portrait of impending doom stands in stark contrast to Ronald Reagan's cheery message of "morning in America." However, while his message can be described as fascistic, what is lacking is the organizational might of "a mass-based party of committed nationalistic militants." In other words, Grey thinks that the potential strongman is there, but the organizational apparatus is not in place for the emergence of a genuine fascist movement (Grey, 2016).

Commentators in various mainstream newspapers and magazines, such as Alexandra Alter in *The New York Times*, have pointed to critics' anxiety about Trump's political proclivities that have triggered a renewed interest in dystopian novels. One in particular has risen to the top of best seller lists: George Orwell's *1984*. Among the books widely mentioned are a few explicitly about America. The threat of fascism is the theme of two novels published nearly 70 years apart. It was first depicted in satirical form shortly after Hitler had gained political control in Germany in Sinclair Lewis's 1935 novel *It Can't Happen Here*. The main character of the novel is thought to be modeled after Louisiana's autocratic populist politician Huey Long. Philip Roth's *The Plot against America*, published in 2004, offers a counterfactual historical novel in which Charles Lindberg, aviator and Nazi sympathizer, beats incumbent Franklin Delano Roosevelt for the presidency in 1940. The question posed in both books was what an American, as opposed to its European counterparts, fascist leader would look like.

It is not necessary to get deep into the weeds about the debate between commentators who have concluded or dissented from the assertion that Trump is a fascist (he himself is on record as disavowing the alt-right) to realize that the very fact that the question has been repeatedly raised reflects widespread anxiety about the threat he is seen by some to pose, not simply to the functioning of a political system, but to democratic culture. How that translates into the fascist equation will not concern us further here, instead turning to the language that has been put to used far more widely and less subject to polemics: right-wing populism. We will turn to expressions of populism in the American electorate in the following chapter. Here we contain the discussion to Trump's politics, reflected primarily in the way he conducted his campaign. Trump's political views have proven to be difficult to pin down, which has led some biographers, including Tony Schwartz, to assume that Trump can't be identified with any particular ideology. One can understand how such a conclusion could be made. First, he has made a half-dozen or more shifts of party affiliation over the years, moving between the two major parties and flirting with the Reform Party initially headed by Ross Perot. Second, he has changed his opinion on any number of hot-button issues, none more fraught than abortion. Third, like his father, he courted politicians, providing campaign contributions — and as Trump himself put it, "when you give, they do whatever the hell you want them to do" (Fahrenthold & Helderman, 2016).

Trump's initial forays into politics had the appearance of testing the waters — something he was encouraged to do by Roger Stone, a close associate of Roy Cohn who has been involved in Republican party operation, with a reputation for hardball tactics, since the Nixon era. In 1987, Trump took out an advertisement in a few major newspapers addressed to "the American people," complaining that the United States was "getting ripped off" by allies in its defense commitments — a complaint that reappeared in the 2016 campaign, this time with a specific attack on NATO members (D'Antonio, 2016, pp. 181–182). He also began his longstanding complaint about American trade deals with other nations — the Japanese in the 1980s — refocused today in particular on China and Mexico.

In 1989, Trump again took out newspaper advertisements, this time in New York City's four major papers. He was reacting to the five black teenagers who were convicted of a vicious rape and beating of a female jogger in Central Park (the conviction was later overturned). Echoing the tabloid press, his advertisement condemned the "roving bands of wild criminals" and in bold headline urged the state to, "BRING BACK THE DEATH PENALTY." He wrote, "I want to hate these muggers and murderers. They should be forced to suffer." He concluded by stating that criminals must learn that their "CIVIL LIBERTIES END WHEN AN ATTACK ON OUR SAFETY BEGINS!"

Trump's critics saw these forays into politics as evidence that it was not likely that he would be seen as a serious candidate because his views were simplistic, uninformed, and, in the second instance, vicious. They questioned whether he had a grasp on democratic political processes and an understanding of the rule of law. However, during the course of the campaign, especially as it became clear that he might actually win the Republican nomination, more concerted efforts were undertaken to come to terms with Trump's political worldview. In the groves of academe, attention turned in some quarters to Nazi political philosopher Carl Schmitt, whose "concept of the political" argued that politics cannot be grounded in rationality, as democratic theorists would like to believe, but rather must be construed as a struggle for power pitting friends against enemies. Rather than the democratic notion of the political sphere as an arena where people wrestle with competing visions of the good life, and do so not as enemies, but as opponents deserving of respect, Trump's political vision is one of winning at all costs and vanquishing "disgusting" enemies. Over a quarter of a century before the 2016 election, the late Edward Shils, then a sociologist at the University of Chicago and Cambridge University, wrote a short essay on "The Virtue of Civil Society" in which he argued that virtue — which he also called civility and public spirit — is essential for a "well-ordered" versus a "disordered liberal democracy." He went on to explicitly respond to Schmitt's idea of a society pitting friends and enemies, writing, "This is true of societies which are on the verge of or are already engaged in civil war. This is the antithesis of civil society" (Shils, 1991, p. 3).

Many other opponents of Trump did not have to reflect on a Nazi theorist to conclude that Trump's is a politics of resentment and anger, lacking an idea of the commonweal. In his acceptance speech on election night, he said, "Now it's time for America to bind the wounds of division; have to come together [sic]. ... I say it is time for us to come together as one united people." Given how divisive his campaign had been and due to the very way he presented these comments, many of those critics heard them more as a threat to opponents than a reaching out to them. It is not surprising that days after the election, the Pew Research Center found that only 30% of voters were prepared to give his campaign an A or B grade for the way it had been conducted — compared, for example, to the 75% given to Barack Obama in 2008 (cited in Blow, 2016).

Right-wing populism and fascism are perhaps two terms describing essentially the same phenomenon. However, whereas the latter suggests the dangerous intrusion of an outside force into a democracy, as Princeton politics professor Jan-Werner Müller persuasively argues, the former comes "from within the democratic world," not as a purer form of democracy, but rather as "a form of politics that is blatantly antidemocratic." Echoing Eco's view of fascism, Müller does not see populism as exhibiting "anything like a codified doctrine," but rather operates with what he calls "an inner logic" (Müller, 2016, pp. 6–10).

In specifying the key elements of that inner logic, analysts typically begin with the idea that populism pits corrupt elites against a pure people (Akkerman, Mudde, & Zaslove, 2014, pp. 1326–1327). Elites are typically depicted as not only corrupt, but as inept and as failures in terms of meeting the needs of the people, while the people are portrayed as victims of elites. This was a recurring theme of Trump's campaign, which sought to contrast him as not only a successful businessman, but as an outsider to the political establishment who, despite his wealth and his lifetime of living in New York City, was in touch with the needs and desires of ordinary people in the American heartland. But expressions of anti-elitism extended beyond condemning political elites. Thus, for example, in defiance of the scientific community's overwhelming consensus about the human impact on global climate change, he became a spokesperson for those declaring global warming a hoax. His anti-elitist stance extended to media, social policy, and intellectual elites. Critics argue that this fits into a characteristic feature of populism that makes it antithetical to democracy, the distinction summarized in sociologist Ralf Dahrendorf's pithy contrast, "populism is simple; democracy is complex" (cited in Müller, pp. 2–16).

The second characteristic feature of right-wing populism's inner logic is its exclusionary view of who constitutes "the people." In this regard, Müller observes, it is "always *antipluralist*," and as such it "is always a *form of identity politics*." Trump's version of nationalism has been portrayed by critics as a textbook example of such antipluralism. For example, during the election, Trump portrayed Mexican immigrants as rapists and murderers who stole American jobs when they weren't busy committing crimes: people who would be kept out by the promise of a large and impenetrable wall extending the entire length of the Mexican–U.S. border. In fact, the idea of building a wall across the entire U.S.–Mexico border was part of Trump's boilerplate campaign speech rhetoric, and it came under sustained criticism from academics, pundits, and late night television comics such as Stephen Colbert and Seth Meyers. The imagery of the wall was linked in his speeches to the erosion of the nation itself. Unless we secure our borders, he argued, we will lose any sense of what it means to be an American. And playing on fears of terrorism, he called for stopping all Muslims from entering the country, advocating for something he described as "extreme vetting" and persisting in his claim that he had seen thousands of Muslims in Jersey City cheering as the World Trade Center towers came down on 9/11. In a *New York Times* column, Jonathan Martin and Alexander Burns pointedly linked his anti-Muslim views to an antipluralistic political worldview, contending that his response to the

Orlando nightclub massacre in June, 2016, amounted to "tossing pluralism aside" by refusing to distinguish "between mainstream Muslims and Islamic terrorists," and accusing the former of being "complicit in acts of domestic terrorism for failing to report attacks in advance."

In this regard, alarm bells were raised by opponents that the dangers of Trump's particular identity politics were evident via what was viewed as connections to white supremacist groups, some of whom have sought to rebrand themselves as the "alt-right" in an effort to get a foothold in the mainstream. Although Trump has publicly disavowed the alt-right, his decision to bring Steve Bannon, who as the head of Breitbart News described the operation as providing a platform for the alt-right, into the White House is depicted in this counter-narrative as reflecting his constricted definition of "the people." If much of the rhetoric has been about excluding the Other, when describing who he claimed to represent, Trump at times has channeled Richard Nixon by referring to them as the silent majority. Speaking of this presumed voiceless constituency, he said at a rally in May, 2016, "the only important thing is the unification of the people — because the other people don't mean anything" (quoted in Müller, 2016, p. 23).

Müller adds one further feature of right-wing populism's inner logic, which is the prevalence of conspiracy theories. This is not, he contends, coincidental, but a vital aspect of efforts to portray the system as a fraud — and thus to delegitimize it. As has become increasingly evident to a large swath of the public, Trump's reliance on charges of conspiracy is extreme by any standards. They include his preparation for losing the election by claiming the vote had been rigged. His reliance on fake-news sources is by now widely recognized, leading some to talk about the prospect of entering an era in which the nation is ruled by a post-truth President.

When Trump gave a speech written by Bannon to an audience of supporters in West Palm Beach weeks before the election, he used what could be interpreted as anti-Semitic tropes dating to the Protocols of the Elders of Zion (the anti-Semitic screed that first appeared in czarist Russia) by asserting that "Hillary Clinton meets in secret with international bankers to plot the destruction of US sovereignty in order to enrich these global financial powers, her special interest friends, and her donors." Journalist Mark Danner attended the rally and described the crowd's response, "The cheers in the hall were deafening, punctuated by ferocious chants of 'Treason' and 'CNN Sucks!' directed at the reporters present." This is the base — ill-informed, angry, and intimidating. To what extent this description characterizes those who voted for Trump on November 8 more broadly is the question we explore in the next chapter.

WORKING THE BINARIES

The performance of politics in the electoral process of liberal democracies calls for the creation of narratives and counter-narratives that seek to depict candidates as civil or uncivil. Campaigns attempt to portray their candidate as imbued with civil virtues while casting the opponent as in some ways insufficiently virtuous to deserve the support of voters. This is what Jeffrey C. Alexander calls "working the binaries." This chapter has explored the three parallel, but ultimately intertwined, anti-Trump narratives that have taken hold, elements of which were deployed throughout the campaign to discredit Trump in an effort to convince voters that he did not deserve their votes. What makes these anti-Trump narratives distinctive is twofold. First, they appear far more robust, containing considerably more specificity than is typical. A summary look at the uncivil vices listed in **Table 2.1** reveals that, uncharacteristic of previous Presidential campaigns, each item on the list is addressed in some fashion. This leads to the second distinctive feature, which is that rather than being seen simply as an opponent who does not measure up when compared to the alternative, the anti-Trump narratives seem to raise far deeper concerns about fitness, concerns that have led many opponents to question what a Trump administration says about the state of American democracy, and what it might mean for the future of the culture necessary to sustain it.

These narratives did not percolate deeply enough into the electorate to prevent Trump from being elected. The following two chapters explore some of the main reasons for that outcome. However, this is not to say that they did not have an impact and that they do not continue to live on.

CHAPTER 3

THE TRUMP VOTER: LABELING THE BASKETS

In a speech delivered at the LGBT for Hillary Gala in New York City on September 9, 2016, Hillary Clinton characterized Trump voters in part in terms that drew a firestorm of criticism from many of those very supporters. What became the take-away for many in the media and for the Trump camp was when she said that, "you could put half of Trump's supporters into what I call the basket of deplorables. Right? The racist, sex-ist, homophobic, xenophobic, Islamaphobic — you name it." But the critics failed to take her comments in context or in their entirety. In terms of context, she was responding to Trump's "latest outrageous, offensive, and inappropriate comments" and reacting to what she cast as a "volatile political environment," prefacing her categorization as being "grossly generalistic."

But what was missing from most reporting on the speech was what she went on to say, which was that in another bas-ket there were "people who feel that the government has let them down, the economy has let them down, nobody cares about them, nobody worries about what happens to their lives and their futures, and they're just desperate for change."

She went on to say that, "Those are people we have to understand and empathize with as well" (quoted in Holan, 2016).

While Clinton's use of the word baskets may have been
unusual, her attempt to categorize voters is not. Indeed, in
trying to make sense of what happened on Election Day
Clinton supporters have given voice to their understanding of
the various categories of Trump voters on social media, usually constructing unflattering categories. Thus, one elderly
Midwestern woman who longed to see the first woman
elected to the presidency in her lifetime offered on Facebook
the following categories: (1) the vulnerable or those who
think or feel they are vulnerable; (2) the gullible; (3) the
bigots; (4) the greedy; and (5) the Hillary Haters.

The problem with such categories is that they are not
mutually exclusive. People can be both racists and worried
about their futures, and can be both vulnerable and greedy.
It's possible that a person voted for Trump for one singular
reason, or it may be because of multiple issues or concerns. It
may be that they saw Trump as a charismatic figure who
could lead the nation out of the wilderness. They may have
embraced him as a chaos candidate who would smash the
system. What this chapter will do is to separate the issue of
who voted for Trump based on the data gathered since the
election from the major reasons they lent their support. But
before doing so, this voting bloc needs to be placed into a
larger context, one that appreciates the fact that although
successful in electing their candidate, they are in fact a minority of the adult population.

THE OUTCOME

Donald Trump's electoral victory could not have been
achieved simply by the fact that 62,979,636 voters cast their

ballots for him. Indeed, in a more democratic society — one in which the principle of one person, one vote means that every citizen is able to cast a ballot of equal value to the ballots of every other citizen — Hillary Clinton would be the 45th President of the United States, having received 65,844,610 votes. In other words, the loser of the 2016 election received 48.2% of the vote total, while the winner received 46.1% (Wasserman, 2017).

The reason for this outcome, of course, is the existence of the Electoral College, a mechanism for electing the President and Vice-President that was established by the adoption of Article II, Section I of the US Constitution. The College was created before political parties came into their own, and thus prior to political campaigns. But more significantly, it reflected deep suspicions about the capacity of a majority of ordinary citizens to be sufficiently educated and capable of rational decision-making to make popular democracy viable. When the Republic was founded, the franchise was extended almost solely to white men who were property owners (there were slight variations since states had discretion in determining voter eligibility). Moreover, it was intended to shore up the Southern slavocrats, with the "three-fifths compromise" authored by the slave-owning James Madison designed to insure that white Southerners' votes counted for more than their Northern counterparts, while simultaneously denying slaves voting rights (Kelkar, 2016). The history of the nineteenth and twentieth centuries is one of the ongoing political struggles resulting in growing inclusivity, expanding the boundaries of who is to be accorded the full rights of citizenship. This began first with nonproperty owning white men, then with African Americans in the aftermath of the Civil War, and after World War I the women's suffrage movement finally met with success (Kivisto & Faist, 2007, pp. 15–48).

In this process of inclusion, the limiting democratic ideal reflected in the Electoral College was often noted but ignored as long as the electoral vote and the popular vote were in sync. In 1824, Andrew Jackson actually beat John Qunicy Adams in both electoral and popular vote totals, but not having received a majority of the Electoral College votes, the House of Representatives decided the election in Adams's favor. This is not the issue at hand in the 2016 election, but the elections of 1876 and 1888 were cases in which the winner of the popular vote was denied the presidency.

This would not happen again for over a century, which is perhaps the primary reason that sustained challenges to the Electoral College system as antithetical to democracy were never mounted. Author William Petrocelli penned a guest editorial in a San Francisco newspaper in 1996 raising concern about the potential for systemic unfairness that was treated with derision or yawns at the time. However, when he recently observed that in comparing the number of citizens an elector in low-density Wyoming represents versus one in highly populated California — the disparity is 3.6 to 1 — growing opposition to the Electoral College has become evident. That attention has been sufficient to provoke Bill O'Reilly, a Trump supporter from Fox News, to offer the following condemnation of critics, contending that the "left wants power taken away from the white establishment. They want a profound change in the way America is run" — a rather remarkable defense of the system that denies genuine political equality among citizens in explicitly racial terms (quoted in Bump, 2016).

The contested 2000 election in which the Supreme Court intervened to stop a limited recount in Florida led to George Bush's victory in that state, the overall result being that he beat Al Gore by 271 to 266 electoral votes. Despite this controversial outcome, Gore won the popular vote nationally by over 500,000 votes. This puts the 2016 election into perspective. Trump was awarded 304 Electoral College votes to Clinton's 232. While this was a larger margin than the extremely tight 2000 election, in fact Trump's margin of victory placed him at number 46 in a list of the 58 elections held over the nation's history — not the landslide described by Trump and his spokespersons. The three states that led to this result were Pennsylvania, Ohio, and Michigan, with the sum total vote difference between the candidates in these three states being approximately 110,000, a slim margin. Moreover, that margin was less than the number of votes cast in these three states for Green Party candidate Jill Stein.

What makes the outcome all the more remarkable is that Clinton won the popular vote by 2.9 million votes, which is anything but a slim margin. Trump's response to his popular vote loss in the days immediately after the election was to state that he could have won that vote, too, but didn't seek to do so. However, his pride being injured by the steady stream of post-election commentary on the popular vote totals led him to falsely assert that millions of votes for Clinton were cast illegally in three states that she won, thus suggesting that he was the actual winner of the popular vote (Seipel, 2016).

But simply contrasting, the vote difference between the two candidates overstates the actual electoral support for Trump. In addition to Clinton's 2.9 million vote advantage over Trump, 7,804,213 votes were cast for other candidates, primarily for Libertarian candidate Gary Johnson and Jill Stein (Wasserman, 2017). This amounted to 5.7% of total votes, which when combined with Clinton's percentage advantage over Trump means that non-Trump votes exceeded Trump votes by nearly 8%.

However, even while this indicates that among those who went to the polls, a majority of voters did not vote for Trump, in itself it misses the larger picture. In 2016, the US Census Bureau estimated the total population to be 323,127,513, of which 77.1% were 18 years of age or older — or in other words of voting age. This amounts to a figure of 249,131,313, according to the US Bureau of the Census. However, not all of these people are eligible to vote for various reasons determined at the state level. This includes 6.1 million individuals with felony convictions prohibited from voting, along with those judged to be mentally incompetent or who have not met residency requirements. It's worth noting that given the fact that racial minorities are disproportionately impacted by felon disenfranchisement laws, they serve as a tool for voter suppression resulting in lowering the number of eligible minority voters (Uggen, Larson, & Shannon, 2016).

The total number of votes cast in the presidential election was 136,628,413. If this number is subtracted from the 18 and over population total, 112,502,900 adults did not vote. While estimates vary slightly, in determining the number of these individuals who were actually eligible to vote there is a consensus that the figure is in the range of 95 million, which means that voter turnout in 2016 was 57.9%. This reflects a long pattern in the United States, where voter turnout has not exceeded 60% since 1968. And in fact the 2016 turnout level reflects an increase from 2012 and a level similar to Barack Obama's initial victory in 2008. In 2012, the United States ranked 27 on the list of the 35 member Organization for Economic Cooperation and Development (OECD) countries in terms of the percentage of eligible voters who cast ballots in their country's most recent national election. Only two wealthy countries — Japan and Switzerland — ranked lower (Desilver, 2016).

The Pew Research Center's 2012 demographic profile of nonvoters found that they tend to be younger, less educated, less affluent, and less likely to be married than voters.

Hispanics are more likely to be nonvoters than Anglos. Nonvoters are more likely to indicate no religious affiliation compared to voters. In his 2016 study of "men without work," economist Nicholas Eberstadt found that males outside of the labor force are disinclined to be civically engaged, which includes a disinclination to vote. African Americans and individuals who have spent time in prison — and these two categories obviously intersect — are disproportionately located in the category of men without work.

What makes these nonparticipants problematic for the Democratic Party is that they tend to express liberal views on domestic policy issues, including support for the Affordable Care Act and for a more progressive income tax. They endorse a more activist government than voters as a whole. Their foreign policy views reflect greater opposition to an ongoing military presence in the Middle East and a desire to solve problems diplomatically rather than militarily. At the same time, their views on issues such as abortion, same-sex marriage, and immigration are in sync with voters. Thus, if they were mobilized and energized to vote, the Democratic Party would benefit.

Why people opt not to vote involves a complex set of issues related to external barriers to voting versus individual dispositions to vote (Harder & Krosnick, 2008). The former includes but is not limited to factors such as the ease of registering to vote, quality of information regarding the voting process, ease of access to polling places, the number of polling places, and the prospect of voter intimidation. In this regard, it is worth noting 14 states had passed new restrictive voting laws since the Supreme Court's decision to repeal the provision of the 1965 Voting Rights Act that required federal approval of changes to state election laws. These restrictive measures have a disproportionately negative impact on minority voters (Regan, 2016). Despite claims to the contrary, the goal of these laws is to suppress the minority vote. Just what impact they had on the outcome of the 2016 election is difficult to determine at this point. In terms of individual dispositions, researchers point to the salience of certain demographic variables such as education, income, occupation, age, and gender. In addition, such factors as levels of trust in others, a feeling of political efficacy, a sense of group solidarity, and a belief in civic duty influence decisions about whether or not to vote.

WHAT DO VOTERS KNOW?

Our concern below will not be with analyzing non-Trump voters or nonvoters, but with the 27.1% of the country's eligible voters who opted to vote for Trump. But before focusing attention on them, another aspect of the larger context involves considering what it is that voters in general know. From the founding of American democracy, concerns have been raised about the level of knowledge of the electorate. Indeed, one of the rationales for limiting the franchise was that the least knowledgeable among the citizenry needed to be excluded from making political decisions at the ballot box lest reason give way to irrational impulses (Hochschild, 2010). The felt need for an informed electorate has deep roots in the democratic tradition, as writer Caleb Crain has recently noted, pointing as far back as to Plato, whose preference was for decision-making by "educated guardians" (read: elites). And yet the trajectory of American democracy — like all liberal democracies — has been for the expansion of the franchise, which presumably means that the level of voter knowledge correspondingly declines. The only two remaining categories of citizens for whom voting as a fundamental right is denied are those with felony convictions and some people with intellectual and developmental disabilities.

We have known with considerable empirical detail, since the publication in 1960 of a book by Angus Campbell and his University of Michigan colleagues titled *The American Voter*, that the American electorate is uninformed in many ways, including lacking knowledge about who the relevant political actors — including elected officials and political parties — are at any moment in time and about the central issues of the day, but also about the fundamentals of the way the political system works. Harvard Professor Jennifer L. Hochschild has observed, for example, that a distressingly large percentage of the American electorate in the 1950s Cold War era "thought the Bill of Rights was written recently by Communists," while Crain observed that today, after the demise of Communism, a third of American voters "think that the Marxist slogan 'From each according to his ability to each according to his need' appears in the Constitution." Hochschild is right that "the parlor game of 'dunce cap nation' can be exaggerated and mean-spirited," but this does not call into question the conclusion that Americans "are ignorant of politically salient information" (Crain, 2016, p. 67; Hochschild, 2010, p. 112).

While it is easy to compile a long list of evidence to support this assessment, we will settle for one recent example. According to the Pew Research Center, 57% of voters in 2016 thought that crime had gotten worse during the years of the Obama administration, even though the rate of violent crime continues a more than two-decade decline and was at a historic low point. In this regard, the perceptual divide along political lines is pronounced, with 78% of Trump supporters thinking crime has worsened, but only 37% of Clinton supporters agreeing (Gramlich, 2016a). Similar discrepancies between perceptions and empirical reality can be found in such matters as Mexican immigration rates since 2008, the crime rate of immigrants versus citizens, the number of Muslims residing in the country, and the number of refugees the United States admits each year. These differences, it's worth noting, pertain not to differing evaluations, such as how far the country has come in terms of addressing racial equality, but rather to false perceptions versus reality.

Despite Donald Trump's repeated resending of tweets that originated in the fringes of the extremist right and his decision to bring Steve Bannon into the White House, a month after the election, 54% of Americans said they had not heard anything about the "alt-right movement," while another 26% claimed to know only a little about it. The Pew Research Center survey on the topic found substantial differences in levels of familiarity based on educational attainment. At one end, 76% of individuals with graduate-level college backgrounds were familiar with the alt-right, compared to only 34% of individuals with high school degrees or less. Similarly, 66% of self-defined liberals were aware of the movement, compared to only 44% of self-described conservatives (Gramlich, 2016b).

In a survey of the literature on political knowledge conducted over a decade ago, Professor of Communication, Michael X. Delli Carpini, contended that the typical American voter is poorly informed, but not uninformed. Furthermore, the level of political knowledge has remained quite constant over the course of a half century, despite the fact that more Americans have higher levels of educational attainment today than in the past. The average American is less informed than counterparts in other comparable countries. To what extent this lack of civic knowledge represents a threat to the well-being of a democratic society has been a matter of debate for decades, but few can dispute Delli Carpini's contention that "democracy becomes more responsive and responsible the more informed, and the more equitably informed, is its citizenry" (Delli Carpini, 2005, pp. 27–37).

Further confounding matters, the growth of fake news has become so evident that pundits have taken to talking about living in a post-truth age. As anyone who has stood in the check-out line of any American supermarket can attest when confronted with this week's issue of the *National Enquirer*, fake news is nothing new. But, due to the new social media, rumors and made-up news can spread like wildfire. It can involve embracing false rumors that can readily be proven false, such as claims that Barack Obama is a Muslim, a belief the Pew Research Center concluded had been embraced by 12% of the American electorate when he was elected to office in 2008. In the 2016 election, the number of fake news items increased exponentially. Two examples will suffice. Pope Francis, gullible readers learned, had decided to endorse Trump for President, while Hillary Clinton and her campaign chairperson John Podesta were accused of running a pedophile ring in a backroom of a Washington, DC pizzeria. Because of the persistence and volume of fake news, the efforts of established media outlets to challenge such reports have proven to be an increasingly onerous task.

According to a post-election survey conducted by the Pew Research Center, nearly two-thirds of Americans think that fake news is causing "a great deal of confusion" (only 11% of those surveyed thought it created little or no confusion). Around 85% of these respondents are somewhat or very confident that they can sort out fake from real news, and thus the confusion that they point to would presumably be a problem for other people but not for themselves. About a quarter of respondents admitted to forwarding fake news on to someone else, some intentionally and some unintentionally (Barthel, Mitchell, & Holcomb, 2016).

THE POLARIZATION OF THE ELECTORATE

One of the recurring narratives of contemporary American politics is that the public has become increasing polarized, which is reflected in basic demographic profiles of the two major political parties. The Republican Party is increasingly a party of an aging white electorate, heavily concentrated in rural areas, and embracing conservative religious beliefs — chiefly fundamentalist Protestant. It is also a party whose members exhibit a decreasing educational attainment level compared to the population as a whole. Meanwhile, the Democratic Party is increasingly racially diverse, urban, with higher educational attainment levels than the general public, and inclined to either be secular or embrace liberal religious views.

In a 2014 report, the Pew Research Center (2014a) found that "Republicans and Democrats are more divided along ideological lines — and partisan antipathy is deeper and more extensive — than at any point in the last two decades." It goes on to say that "'Ideological silos' are common on both the left and right. People with down-the-line ideological positions — especially conservatives — are more likely than others to say that most of their close friends share their political views." That being said, taken together the ideologically consistent constitute only around 1 in 5 Americans. Polarization along party lines is paralleled by polarization between more and less educated Americans, with those who have college degrees being most inclined to express consistently liberal views, while those with high school educations or less exhibit the most consistently conservative beliefs. Similarly, there is a growing generational divide, with 45% of the youngest cohort, millennials (those born after 1980), expressing consistently or mostly liberal views, versus 40% of the oldest generation, the silent generation (born between

1928 and 1945) holding consistently or mostly conservative views (Pew Research Center, 2016a).

However, it is important not to arrive at false equivalencies between self-defined liberals and conservatives. In one critical area, the idea of residing in an ideological silo is an apt characterization only for conservatives, and that has to do with media habits. Conservatives rely overwhelmingly on Fox News for political information, while liberals make use of a wide variety of sources the most widely used being NPR, MSNBC, and *The New York Times*. But more significantly, a reflection of the reactionary and paranoid conspiracy-theory framework shaping those who are consistently conservative, the other sources that they trust besides Fox includes Breitbart and the Drudge Report, along with television or radio programs hosted by Glenn Beck, Sean Hannity, and Rush Limbaugh. The only mainstream conservative venue they trust is *The Wall Street Journal*, this being the only print news source they mention, except for three British media sources, the BBC, *The Economist*, and *The Guardian*, which they claim to about equally trust and distrust (given the left-of-center orientation of the third on this list, it's reasonable to question how familiar the respondents actually are about these news sources).

The point is that they distrust all but the one mainstream source noted above, including newspapers such as *The New York Times* and *The Washington Post*, *The New Yorker* magazine, along with broadcasting organizations including ABC, CBS, NBC, CNN, MSNBC, NPR, and PBS. In stark contrast, their consistently liberal opposites have trust in most sources, and in this regard their views are shared to very great extent with not only those described as mostly liberal, but also those in the center identified as mixed. Those who are mostly conservative share more in common with their consistently conservative counterparts than with those in the center (Pew Research Center, 2014b).

Turning to the run-up to the 2016 election, and given that Independents make up a substantial percentage of the electorate, in examining the polarization shaping the outcome of the election, it is useful to look at differences between self-defined Clinton versus self-defined Trump supporters rather than simply between Democrats and Republicans. 81% of Trump supporters think that life for people like them is worse today than it was a half century ago, compared to only 19% of Clinton supporters. Their views of race relations are similarly divergent. Thus, while 78% of Clinton supporters think that white privilege exists, only 24% of Trump supporters agree. 55% of Clinton supporters think that racial discrimination is the main reason blacks can't get ahead, a view shared by only 6% of Trump supporters. In terms of their views on immigration, 79% of Trump supporters favor building a wall along the Mexican border, compared to only 10% of Clinton supporters. Turning to the perceived threat of terrorism, 66% of Trump supporters think that the threat of a terrorist attack is greater today than it was on 9/11, a view to which only 24% of Clinton backers concurred. In turning to gender inequality, whereas 72% of Clinton supporters believe that significant obstacles remain that make it harder for women to get ahead than men, only 31% of Trump supporters agreed. While 70% of Clinton supporters consider the gap between the rich and poor to be a very big problem, only 31% of Trump supporters concur. And finally, while for neither side does a majority of supporters consider the environment to be a very big problem, there is a considerable gap — 43% of Clinton supporters think it is, contrasted to only 16% of Trump supporters (Pew Research Center, 2016b).

WHO VOTED FOR TRUMP?

A demographic profile based on exit polls of who voted for Trump conducted by Edison Research for the National Election Pool points to the major divides within the American electorate. First, race mattered, and it mattered in a big way. Whereas 58% of whites voted for Trump, 29% of both Hispanics and Asians did so, and only 8% of blacks did. Second, gender mattered, though not in as pronounced a way as with race: 53% of males voted for Trump compared to 42% of women (Gould & Harrington, 2016).

One of the recurring narratives explaining Trump support focused on the white working class, these narratives generally implying that lower income voters constituted his voter base. However, both before and after the election there were analysts, including Nate Silver, who argued that educational attainment and not income was the actual variable differentiating Trump and Clinton backers. Indeed, Clinton received a majority of the vote from voters earning under $50,000 per year, while Trump won in every income category from $50,000 upward. The wealthiest voters voted for Trump, but by close margins. Thus, those earning between $100,000 and $249,999 provided Trump with a 1% victory margin, while for those earning more than that the difference was 2%. The income category in which the Trump margin was the greatest was between $50,000 and $99,999. This finding corroborates reports based on primary voters that the median income of Trump voters was approximately $72,000, which, as Nate Silver pointed out, is "lower than the $91,000 median for Kasich. But it's well above the national median household income of about $56,000. It's also higher than the median income for both Hillary Clinton and Bernie Sanders supporters, which is around $61,000 for both" (Gould & Harrington, 2016; Silver, 2016a, 2016b).

When turning to educational attainment, exit polls divided voters into four categories: high school or less, some college/ associate degree, college graduate, and postgraduate study. For the first two categories, Trump won a majority of votes, with the margin being greatest — by 9 points — among some college/associate degree. Among college graduates, Clinton did not gain a majority, but her 49% bested Trump's 45%. It was with people who had pursued postgraduate study that the difference was most pronounced, with Clinton beating Trump by a 58% to 37% margin (Gould & Harrington, 2016).

In comparing Trump's performance to Mitt Romney's four years earlier, economics writer Andrew Flowers examined vote differences at the county level and found that Trump out performed Romney in counties that were older, primarily white, with few immigrants, and with a less educated population than the nation as a whole. This dovetails with two voter differences, the first of which has received less commentary than one might have expected, which is voting by age groups. In this regard, a majority of those between the ages of 18 and 39 voted for Clinton, while the reverse was true of voters 40 and older. This is related to the second difference, which is between urban and rural voters. One thing is clear, the rural/urban divide is pronounced. Whereas 59% of voters in cities over 50,000 voted for Clinton, 62% voted for Trump (including a majority of women) in small cities and rural communities. However, rural voters constitute only 17% of the electorate, while the urban vote, at 34% is twice as large. But this means that the largest voter bloc resides in the suburbs. The 49% of voters who reside in suburbs favored Trump over Clinton by a 50% to 45% margin (Flowers, 2016).

Finally, religion played a role in Trumps' victory. Of particular significance, conservative white Protestants voted overwhelmingly for Trump, by a margin of 81% to 16% (Markoe, 2016). While white Catholics and Mormons also favored Trump, their vote was around 20 points lower than conservative Protestants. This group constitutes the largest segment of the American Christian religious landscape, one that grew from the 1960s into the megachurch era, in contrast to more liberal mainline Protestant denominations, which have steadily declined during that same time period. A body of literature emerged in the sociology of religion from the 1960s through the 1990s that sought to explain why conservative churches were growing, while liberal ones were declining. Buoyed by its expanding membership, the Christian Right became an increasingly assertive political force and aggressively expanded its broadcast programming, its presence in higher education, and its influence in statehouses around the nation and in the corridors of power in Washington, DC.

However, in the twenty-first century, the trend line for conservative churches has turned in the opposite direction. In a widely discussed 2015 study, the Pew Research Center found a downward trend line between 2007 and 2014 for evangelical Protestants, Catholics, and mainline Protestants — a total combined decline of 7.4%. At the same time, non-Christian faiths had grown by 1.2% while the unaffiliated grew 6.7%. Although the decline has been gradual, the Pew researchers saw nothing to suggest that it was likely to be turned around in the foreseeable future, which is a source of growing anxiety within what is becoming an aging community. Once confident that they might become a "moral majority," they now confront their old bête noire — secularism.

WHY DID VOTERS SUPPORT TRUMP?

Given Donald Trump's widespread unpopularity in the mainstream media and the concerns raised about his candidacy, expressed in the narratives discussed in Chapter 2, why did tens of millions of Americans vote for him? What did they see in him that differed so greatly from an even larger number of fellow citizens who either voted against him or sat the election out? There is reason to believe that among those who did not cast a ballot for the Republican nominee were the two remaining former Republican Presidents, part of a contingent of life-long members of the party who saw in Trump an existential threat to its future. In attempting to provide insight into Trump voters, some have turned to a literature on the authoritarian personality that dates to the aftermath of the Nazi defeat when questions were raised about how it came to be that fascism had triumphed in Germany and elsewhere in Europe. Among those asking these questions were a group of émigré scholars who had fled Hitler and sought refuge in America.

As Alex Ross put it in a December 2016 *New Yorker* article, "The Frankfurt School Knew Trump Was Coming." He was thinking specifically about a publication that appeared in mid-twentieth century, *The Authoritarian Personality*, whose lead author was the Frankfurt School sociologist Theodor Adorno. This landmark study, funded by the American Jewish Committee, set in motion a decades-long effort to understand the character traits of people who succumbed to the appeal of fascism. The study sought to use insights from psychoanalytic thought to provide a composite portrait of the character type inclined to submit to an autocratic demagogue, while aggressively scapegoating marginalized minority groups. The impetus of the research project, replete with a battery of survey instruments including one called the F-Scale (as in Fascism-Scale), was very much present oriented, seeking to determine whether the United States and similar democracies were inhabited by a sufficient number of potential recruits to movements headed by anti-democratic autocrats. It was this line of thought that motivated subsequent work on the psychology of authoritarianism, some closely aligned to the psychoanalytic tradition, some not — including work by scholars such as Stanley Milgram, Robert Altemeyer, and Alexander Mitscherlich. And despite vigorous insider debates and at times a waning interest in the topic, the idea of the authoritarian personality has never gone away.

On the contrary, in part motivated by the shift on the American right prior to the rise of Trump that saw conventional conservatism losing out to the radical right, a renewal of interest in the authoritarian personality became evident in some social science quarters. Perhaps the most influential book that reflected this interest appeared in 2009, *Authoritarianism and Polarization in American Politics*, by political scientists Marc Hetherington and Jonathan Weiler. They rehabilitated the concept to understand differences on many social issue flashpoints, including same-sex marriage, undocumented immigrants, and race. Stressing differences in child-rearing practices (in simplified terms, spanking versus time-out), like Adorno and his colleagues, Hetherington and Weiler's goal was to get at the deep psychology that underpins and influences political orientations. In their view, concurring with the portrait offered by Adorno and associates, authoritarians differ from nonauthoritarians insofar as they place a premium on order, control, conformity, and obedience.

Authoritarian thinking is characterized by being rigid, simplistic, and exclusionary — viewing the world in terms of stark black-and-white polarities that divide social actors into us-them categories. Karen Stenner's *The Authoritarian Dynamic*, published a few years earlier in 2005, dovetails with the approach of Hetherington and Weiler. In understanding intolerance in action, she stresses the interaction of a personality predisposed to authoritarianism with a perceived threat to one's well-being or way of life; it's when the two come together that political mobilization becomes possible.

While scholars working in this field usually contend that authoritarianism is not necessarily confined to the political right, they also point to the fact that in the current American context, it is only in right-wing politics that the impact of authoritarianism is felt. Given that the radical right has grown numerically as a percentage of Republican Party membership, this party becomes home to most authoritarians. Thus, it is only here that authoritarians have achieved political voice. In making this case, political analysts continue a line of argument that traces back to historian Richard Hofstadter's 1964 article (and subsequent book) on "The Paranoid Style in American Politics." Hofstadter stressed that he was not using the term paranoid in a clinical way, but adopting it to account for the American right wing in the 1950s and 1960s. He had in mind, for example, the conspiratorial nature of Senator Joseph McCarthy's communist purge and the efforts of the John Birch Society to paint the goal of the United Nations as the destruction of US sovereignty, replacing it with a world government.

While Hofstadter focused on the paranoid rhetorical style of various right-wing operatives, he contended that underlying the rhetoric was a sense of being "dispossessed: America has been largely taken away from them and their kind, though they are determined to try to repossess it and to prevent the final destructive act of subversion" (Hofstadter, 1964, p. 81). In Hofstadter's account, the roots of this right-wing paranoid style took off during the New Deal — socialism, in their eyes — and gained traction during the Cold War as justifiable concerns about the Soviet military threat were convoluted with irrational fears that the American way of life was being undermined from within by communist-inspired collectivism. Perhaps the enduring appeal among such minded people of right-wing author Ayn Rand's novels (Speaker of the House Paul Ryan's favorite novelist) is an indication of the persistence and the pervasiveness of reactionary political views.

Hetherington and Weiler found that those groups scoring highest on the authoritarian scale were conservative Protestant churchgoers, residents of small towns, Southerners, and peoples with a high school education or less — and as we have seen this dovetails precisely with the Trump voter profile, this era's manifestation of anti-intellectualism. These constitute, not the entirety, but a core constituency of the Republican Party. In a widely discussed 2016 academic journal article that examined how Trump won the Republican nomination, Matthew C. MacWilliams argues that the crowded candidate pool resulted in party elites failing to coalesce around a more traditional candidate, and this paved the way for someone like Trump, who was perceived to be a political outsider sharing the base's dystopian, us-versus-them worldview. One presumes then that the Never-Trump — non-authoritarian — faction of the Republican Party voted for Hillary, Gary Johnson, or a write-in candidate, or simply sat out the election. Countering this move away from Trump was the shift toward him by authoritarians among the ranks of Independents and Democrats who embraced Trump's right-wing populist vision.

But can authoritarianism account for all of the 62 million people who voted for Trump? Probably not, and nobody has actually suggested as much. But it does cast doubt on the frequently repeated narrative that reduces the Trump voter to the white working class. As Jonathan Weiler reported in a blog post for *The Huffington Post* published in September 2016, "what distinguishes Democratic from Republican voters among whites isn't education level or income level. It's authoritarianism. The data are consistent in this: low-authoritarian white folks with less than a college education, or who earn less than the median income, overwhelmingly support Democrats. Conversely, whites with high incomes and high educational levels but who also score high in authoritarianism strongly support Republicans." Moreover, authoritarianism can potentially account for why it was that 29% of Latinos and Asians, along with 8% of African Americans voted for Trump despite his vilification of racial minorities and immigrants. Here one can reasonably surmise that many of these minority voters are affiliated with fundamentalist Protestant churches, and religion trumped race when they cast their ballots.

Beyond the effort to distinguish Trump voters from the rest of the citizenry is an awareness of the fact that those voters who chose Trump at the ballot box did so for a variety of reasons, and their level of enthusiasm for the candidate likewise ranged from the fervor of the base to considerable skepticism at the other end of the continuum. One might characterize this spectrum as ranging from the "Hail Trump" contingent of white supremacists to the "I held my nose and voted for him" bloc of voters. What this reflects are voters who helped to unleash the politics of cruelty either because they embraced it or because they turned their eyes from it but nevertheless condoned it.

When media commentators turn their attention to the fascists, they are often at pains to note that the movement attracts relatively small numbers. While true, the difficult thing to ascertain is to what extent their views are shared by others who are not necessarily activists. Moreover, given Trump's repeated re-tweets of incendiary messages from this ideological netherworld, he has granted them legitimacy and entitlement. Certainly the event that elicited the greatest amount of attention was a gathering to celebrate the election results in which Richard Spencer gave an impassioned speech. He heads the National Policy Institute, a racist organization devoted to "ensuring the biological and cultural continuity" of the white race. Claiming that he is not a fascist, but an "identitarian," he allegedly, according to a *Washington Post* article by Jonathan Woodrow Cox, exhorted the crowd, "Let's party like it's 1933" and ended the evening with a Nazi salute as the assembled shouted "Hail Trump." The goal of this movement is an all-white ethno-state and in achieving the ethnic cleansing that would eliminate tens of millions of non-whites, Spencer told Woodrow Cox, "maybe it will be horribly bloody and terrible."

According to Keegan Hankes, in a 2017 blog for the Southern Poverty Law Center, an organization dedicated to monitoring the activities of hate groups, there is a division in the ranks of the racist radical right, pitting the alt-right from the "alt-light." The latter are seen by the former as not sufficiently dedicated to creating an authoritarian state and as unwilling to be faithful to 1933 by including a sufficiently virulent version of anti-Semitism into their rhetoric — some of them, for instance, preferring to focus their attacks on feminism. Andrew Marantz's 2016 "Trolls for Trump" profile focused on Mike Cernovich, who made his name as an Internet misogynist dispensing advice such as "Misogyny Gets You Laid" before he parlayed that into a full-throttled assault on Hillary Clinton. He believes that his "first marriage was ruined by feminist indoctrination," and for that reason is of like mind with Milo Yiannopoulos (a darling of the alt-right movement, who was permanently banned from Twitter in July 2016), who published a piece in Breitbart.com titled "Would You Rather Have Feminism or Cancer?"

Among those the purists see as alt-light is Steve Bannon, who served as Trump's campaign CEO and assumed the role of Chief Strategist in the White House. Bannon's promotes a potted version of Roman Catholicism's "church militant" theology. Samuel Freedman reported that in a talk Bannon gave to a group of conservative Catholics in the Vatican in 2014, he "called on the 'church militant' to fight a global war against a 'new barbarity' of 'Islamic fascism' and international financial elites with 2,500 years of Western civilization at risk." Bannon posed the threat to the Christian West as coming from outside — at the Gates of Vienna, as the radical right has it — and the internal machinations of an international Jewish conspiracy, this season's version of the Protocols of the Elders of Zion. At the same time, elsewhere he has bashed the American Catholic Church for being too hospitable to immigrants, while criticizing the social justice message of the church and Pope Francis's critiques of capitalism (Freedman, 2016).

The unprecedented reality is that the most extremist right-wing forces, those routinely condemned across the political spectrum now have been given voice in the corridors of power. Add to this the fact that Bannon is a media person, heading Breitbart.com, who is expanding existing linkages with right-wing populist parties in Europe. In this regard, there is the potential for a sustained propaganda operation that attempts to reach deeper into the Trump voter base to shape their views. The fact that a majority of Americans haven't heard of the alt-right — and that would include a higher percentage of Trump voters versus those on the left — may or may not be particularly reassuring.

In seeking to understand why people not located on the extremist fringe voted for Trump, we turn first to the responses of a group of voters interviewed by *The Guardian's* Carmen Fishwick, who spoke to six individuals the day of the election. The first, identified as a female small business owner from Indiana, expressed hostility to the "Clinton legacy," "the political system," "the media," and "the Democrats." She described herself as part of Middle America, by which she means people who are hardworking and careful about their personal finances. While she claimed not to condone racism or sexism, she liked Trump because he "tells you what he thinks." A retired federal employee from Pennsylvania stressed Trump the businessman. He was convinced that Trump "knows how to make deals, deals that will make American prosperous again." He complained about Obamacare, which he characterized as a failure, and about the Obama administration "flooding us with Syrian refugees."

The major factor that prompted a woman from Florida to vote for Trump was that he would insure that the nation had "conservative laws." In particular, she was fearful of efforts to roll back the Second Amendment and she wanted to see abortion prohibited. Unlike the previous two voters, she made clear that she didn't like Trump. In fact, she said, "I was deeply saddened to vote for him. His personality, his mannerisms, and his experience repulse me." A software engineer from Ohio was preoccupied with the idea that Clinton was a warmonger who would take us "ever closer to a full-scale nuclear war with Russia." Trump was someone who would shake-up the status quo, and unlike Clinton who lies, Trump "is exactly what you get." Curiously, he went on to say that what you get with "Trump is a slimy scumbag." Continuing on, he said, "Countries may be laughing at us but it took some balls to elect Trump last night. I don't think a single person who cast a vote for him felt good about it. I sure didn't, but felt there was no other choice. It was either Trump or guaranteed war."

A woman from New Jersey complained that Obama "has put a wedge between the people of the country" and described Clinton as "tainted." She said the country needs jobs, but didn't suggest that Trump had a plan of action to create jobs. Rather, she liked him because he was an outsider who "won't take nonsense from anyone" and because he is not beholden to special interests. She believed, "He's for the people!" Another female small business owner, this one from Kansas, contended that Trump could revive the American dream and liked what he said about the military, terrorism, and the police. In contrast, Clinton would simply perpetuate all of the redistributive policies of Obama. More than the other interviewees, she had a list of strongly held views: keeping the minimum wage low, lower taxes, cutting welfare benefits, gun rights, and "a halt to the preference of immigrants before citizens."

There is nothing new about this list of political views. They reflect positions long prominent among Republican Party stalwarts. While there have been numerous efforts to provide deeper insights into the life worlds of right-wing Americans, two recent ethnographic accounts stand out: Arlie Russell Hochschild's *Strangers in Their Own Land* and Katherine J. Cramer's *The Politics of Resentment*, both published in 2016. The former takes readers into the world of Tea Party supporters in Louisiana, while the latter looks at the residents of rural Wisconsin who contributed to the political success of Scott Walker.

Hochschild's book, which was shortlisted for the National Book Award, builds on her work on emotions, her desire here to ascertain how "life feels to people on the right." To that end, over the course of a half decade she visited with a small number of people in the Lake Charles area, whom she got to know quite well. They represented a particular segment of the American population that has moved ever further to the right during the past three decades, while nothing comparable has occurred on the left. These people no longer occupy a place in a more traditional right/left mainstream — what was once thought of as the vital center that made possible civility and respect for one's opponents in the process of democratic engagement.

This movement rightward has an emotional valence attached to it, as the book's subtitle indicates, for these people are angry and fearful of what they perceive to be threats to their way of life. Hochschild sought to make sense of the paradoxes of these members of the middle class who embrace a disdain of government, particularly the federal government, while being the beneficiaries of a range of government services. Moreover, despite the fact that they live in one of the nation's five most polluted counties due to the environmental degradation caused by the petroleum industry, they resent efforts by the federal Environmental Protection Agency to crack down on corporate polluters. Because they think that as the source of good jobs, the corporate polluters are a necessary evil, their hostility is not directed at industry, though it is responsible for undermining their way of life, for example, by making rivers and streams too dangerous to fish or swim in.

Hochschild agrees with psychologist Jonathan Haidt that the political worldview of people is shaped to a large extent by particular cultural values, and while both those on the right and the left value caring and fairness, they come to understand those values in concrete terms in very different ways and each side comes to valorize other values differently, with the right giving priority to obedience while the left does the same for originality. She goes on to note that one can "hold a set of values calmly, or in a state of fury," with potentially far-reaching implications for political action when rage takes hold. Hochschild agrees with Harvard's Theda Skocpol and Vanessa Williamson, who concluded in their 2012 book *The Tea Party and the Remaking of Republican Conservatism*, that the events that churned the values of the Tea Party into outrage were threefold: "the Great Recession of 2008 and government efforts to forestall it, the Presidency of Barack Obama, and Fox News."

Hochschild found that the Tea Party adherents she got to know were warm and generous to those they knew — family, friends, neighbors — and could be welcoming to a coastal liberal like her. At the same time, their antipathies were intense, as with Madonna Massey, a gospel singer whose husband runs a megachurch that is so successful that she can afford to live in a "lovely house" and drive a white Mercedes. A devotee of Rush Limbaugh, Madonna shares his contempt for "femi-nazis," "commie libs," and "environmental wackos." Hochschild's subjects complained about tax rates being too high and were uniformly hostile to welfare programs that in their view went to freeloaders. Their view of the welfare state was one in which the have-nots unfairly take from the haves, the lazy from the industrious. In this mindset, major programs that they benefit from such as Social Security and Medicare are not considered to be welfare, but rather programs that they had paid into and thus were owed to them. On the other hand, unaware of the varied ways that the Affordable Care Act impacted the public at large (e.g., preventing health insurance companies from refusing to insure people with pre-existing conditions), it was seen as a program for the takers that was paid for by hardworking people like themselves.

Matching their hostility of political elites was their disdain of intellectual elites. This could be seen in their attitude toward climate science. While some of Hochschild's subjects thought climate change was a hoax, others were prepared to think it was happening, but in explaining why it was happening and how to respond, they turned to fundamentalist Christianity rather than to science for answers. The idea of the rapture was central to some of her interviewees' worldviews, the belief that the destruction of the earth is preordained by God, and that at the end times, the remnant of true believers would be swept up into heaven while the rest of humanity would be eternally damned.

Hochschild was struck by the fact that despite the fact that they lived in an environmental disaster zone, none of the major white churches expressed any concerns about environmental stewardship on their websites. Likewise, there was no evidence among these believers in the inerrancy of the Bible that they took seriously Matthew 25:35–40, Jesus's injunction to care for the poor, the suffering, and the needy — "the least of these brothers and sisters of mine." In Madonna's case, the prosperity gospel shapes her thinking. As Hochschild summarized her attitude about her responsibility for the truly disadvantaged, "With God's help, she believes, everyone can rise as she has, one person at a time, if one truly and completely allows God to strengthen one's resolve." Hochschild concluded that this was a view shared by many conservative Protestants, observing that area churches seemed "to turn away from social problems in Louisiana — poverty, poor schools, pollution-related illness ..."

A flight attendant who through her travels was exposed to a variety of news sources considered all venues except a select number on the right, particularly Fox News and *The Drudge Report*, to reflect nothing but liberal bias. She thought that liberal political correctness was foisted on her to make her feel guilty about the problems of suffering people in poor nations and to step up and do something when "the problems aren't our fault." She thought that liberals were imposing their PC standards about how she should feel about "a sick African child" or a "bedraggled Indian," and she resented the implication that because she didn't care she was "a bad person."

Underlying these attitudes is what Hochschild calls "the deep story," by which she means the subjective lens through which people make sense of the world. She summarizes the collective deep story of these Tea Party partisans in the following way. They have worked hard and played by the rules of the game, and have patiently waited to achieve their version of the American Dream, but unfortunately they confront "line cutters," and thus they rightly feel a deep sense of betrayal. "Blacks, women, immigrants, refugees, brown pelicans [a protected species] — all have cut ahead of you in line." Behind the deep story lie three major and intertwined social divisions in American life: race, gender, and class.

The sense of victimhood runs deep among these people and adding to that feeling is the conviction that those on the left see them as gun-toting, Bible-thumping, racists, sexists, and ignoramuses. Believing they are the victims, even though they are better off economically than many Americans, they have an incapacity to care about the well-being of those in their midst who are less well-off. Mere insensitivity to such concerns has in the Tea Party movement taken on a politics of cruelty. As one man told Hochschild, echoing almost exactly the words of the flight attendant, "People think we're not good people if we don't feel sorry for blacks and immigrants and Syrian refugees. But I am a good person and I *don't* feel sorry for them."

The core of the earth kind of deep story for Southerners involves black–white relations from slavery through Jim Crow to the present. Lake Charles is 50% black, yet the ordinary black fellow citizens of their community appear to be to large extent invisible to Tea Party adherents. Theirs is a world in which race relations are characterized by physical propinquity and social distance. Moreover, their deep story is incongruent with the history of black–white relations, which intersects with hostility to federal government programs in the post-civil rights era that sought to redress the centuries-long legacy of oppression and segregation. Rather than confronting the historical record (including some of the most incisive accounts of this history written by white Southern historians such as C. Van Woodward), the whites of Lake Charles prefer the midnight and magnolia and the lost cause myths. They are unwilling to reckon with the implications of what William Faulkner, that son of the Deep South, once wrote, "The past is never dead. It's not even past."

Thus, while railing against what they see as the unfairness of post-1964 affirmative action programs, they fail to recognize that time, as Columbia University Professor Ira Katznelson puts it, "when affirmative action was white" (Katznelson, 2005). In countless ways, the emergence of the New Deal welfare programs, including early on Social Security, and extending in succeeding decades to such impactful policies as those associated with FHA and VA mortgages, were designed in ways that privileged whites and disadvantaged blacks. Beyond that, they reveal a fundamental incapacity or conscious unwillingness to reckon with the history of Jim Crow, with its century-long success in insuring the domination and segregation of black Southerners.

When we turn to another group of potential Trump voters far from Louisiana, but still in the American heartland, in Katherine Cramer's 2016 ethnography of rural citizens in northern Wisconsin, a similar picture emerges. These are the voters that helped to propel Scott Walker into the governor's mansion in a state that has historically oscillated between the politics of the left and the right. Walker built his reputation in no small part on his aggressive efforts to undermine public sector unions. In so doing, he became the beneficiary of Koch brother's largesse, tapping into the resources of these enormously wealthy right-wing activists. This funding helped him obtain sufficient national recognition to decide to run for the Republican nomination for President.

Cramer discovered that the political universe of her rural Walker supporters was shaped by two factors. First, they saw their world defined primarily in terms of an urban–rural divide. And second, their singular political attitude was one of resentment. Their understanding of their political friends and enemies was constituted more by concerns about identity — rural and white — than by specific issues, and by their conviction that they were victims. Cramer summarized the elements of victimhood as follows: "(1) a belief that rural areas are ignored by decision makers, including policy makers, (2) a perception that rural areas do not get their fair share of resources, and (3) a sense that rural folks have fundamentally distinct values and lifestyles, which are misunderstood and disrespected by city folks."

Fitting the pattern of right-wing populism, their antipathies were geographically inscribed. They disliked Madison, home to the flagship campus of the University of Wisconsin, and they equally disliked Milwaukee. The university represented the institutional base for arrogant liberal academic elites who indoctrinated their students with leftist and secular ideals. Beyond that, anti-intellectualism writ large was evident in their conversations with Cramer. Meanwhile, Milwaukee was associated with blacks, who were seen as generators of costly social problems contributing to high taxes, and as the undeserving beneficiaries of various government programs. There were contextual features that served to differentiate rural Wisconsin from Lake Charles. First, there are very few blacks living in rural Wisconsin, so racist attitudes toward blacks are shaped by their understanding of an abstract Other. At the same time, Native Americans do reside in rural Wisconsin and they, too, are the objects of animosity, motivated in part by resentment about rights articulated in treaties that the indigenous people of the area exercise — such as hunting and fishing rights. And there is evidence of hostility to Hmong refugees who were settled in a few small cities in the state after the Vietnam War.

Like the Tea Party adherents in the bayou, Cramer's subjects saw themselves as hardworking and playing by the rules,
but not being adequately rewarded for their efforts. And both
Southerners and Northerners complained that their tax bills
were too high. This manifested itself differently in a state
with a history of strong labor unions like Wisconsin insofar
as one of the reasons that rural whites supported Scott
Walker was due to his attacks on public sector workers, who
were seen as being overpaid and underworked. Such views
were consonant with the call for small government, a call
that was articulated ambivalently because many of these rural
Wisconsinites depended on and take advantage of a variety
of government programs.

AT LAST, LABELING THE BASKETS

People who voted for Donald Trump are not a homogeneous
group, but what they share is their embrace — sometimes
explicitly, at other times more implicitly; sometimes asser-
tively, sometimes quietly — of the ideology of right-wing
populism. Thus, the two baskets, or what should more precisely be called categorical frameworks, that account for the
way they conceptualize their political world are precisely
those described in the previous chapter: anti-elitism and an
exclusionary view of the people. In this regard, the Trump
phenomenon is the American counterpart to what author and
journalist John Judis has called the "populist explosion" in
Europe. That being said, within this categorical framework
right-wing populism plays out in different national contexts
in distinctive ways reflecting differing histories and demographic compositions.

As will become more evident in the following chapter, but
is present in the discussion contained in the preceding pages,

right-wing populism in the United States did not arrive on the scene with the rise of Trump. In fact, right-wing populism has roots in the Republican Party from at least the 1960s forward. While its influence has waxed and waned over time, moments of crisis such as the Great Recession of 2008 have served to reenergize it, as the birth of the Tea Party attests. In this regard, Trump is merely this season's vessel for reactionary politics.

It is useful to consider how right-wing populists define the people before clarifying their understanding of the elites that they disparage. Since populism is about the people, it is inherently a form of identity politics. In the weeks following the election, as liberals attempted to make sense of what had happened, intellectual historian Mark Lilla cautioned them about overemphasizing the virtues of diversity and what he termed "identity liberalism," pointing to Hillary Clinton's frequent expressions of support for "African-American, Latino, LGBT, and women voters at every stop." Certainly, the right-wing mantra condemning multiculturalism and every other manifestation of what they call PC reveals contempt for such diversity. And from the left there has been a longstanding debate about the priority accorded to the politics of recognition versus the politics of redistribution. Lilla is in the latter camp, speaking as someone intent on seeking to begin the process of the political revitalization of liberalism. His message is worth quoting at length:

> ...*the whitelash thesis is convenient because it*
> *absolves liberals of not recognizing how their own*
> *obsession with diversity has encouraged white, rural,*
> *religious Americans to think of themselves as a dis-*
> *advantaged group whose identity is being threatened*
> *or ignored. Such people are not actually reacting*
> *against the reality of our diverse America (they tend,*

*after all, to live in homogeneous areas of the coun-
try). But they are reacting against the omnipresent
rhetoric of identity, which is what they mean by
"political correctness." Liberals should bear in mind
that the first identity movement in American politics
was the Ku Klux Klan, which still exists. Those who
play the identity game should be prepared to lose it.
(Lilla, 2016)*

The problem with Lilla's argument is that it fails to appreci-
ate the fact that American identity has been the product of
identity politics from the founding of the Republic, when it was
determined that slaves were to be excluded from the benefits of
citizenship while, as a recent Nobel laureate put it, the economic foundation of the nation was simultaneously "founded
on the backs of slaves" (Gilmore, 2012). Moreover, in that
long history, it has always been the disadvantaged and marginalized that have had to combat their stigmatized identities —
precisely those categories of people Clinton kept mentioning. It
was with this in mind that social theorist Erving Goffman over
a half century ago claimed that a "pivotal fact" of that historical moment was that stigmatized persons were making claims
contrary to the damaged identities imposed on them by "nor-
mals," contending instead that they were in fact human beings
"like anyone else." He actually used the term "politics of identity" to describe what was taking place, which, it should be
stressed, was a reactive effort to lay claim to one's identity.
And it should further be noted, as the civil rights and women's
movements attest, this did not preclude pushing a redistributive
agenda (Goffman, 1963, pp. 7, 123).

If right-wing populists weren't motivated by the politics of
identity, but instead were prepared to frame their grievances
in class terms, why didn't they rally around Bernie Sanders —
who, recall, was faulted early in his campaign for failing to

adequately address recognition given his emphasis on redistribution? I suspect one can go far in answering that question by pointing to elements of his identity: he is Jewish, an atheist, and self-proclaimed democratic socialist. Their sense of victimhood is inextricably tied to their hostility to both marginalized populations and to liberals who, in identifying with such populations, are deemed to be perpetrators of PC.

Thus, in depicting how right-wing populists draw the boundaries of "the people," one can think in terms of binary codes that contrast those located within the boundaries from those on the outside, as sociologist Jeffrey C. Alexander has argued. As Table 3.1 summarizes, among the most salient boundary-defining differences demarcating the people are: whites versus non-whites; religious people versus secularists; Christians versus non-Christians; "traditional" women versus feminists; heterosexuals versus LGBTQ people; hardworking individuals versus the lazy; residents of the heartland versus coastal elites; and those dedicated to "free market" capitalism versus advocates of the welfare state, socialists and communists. I will take up this topic in further detail in the following

Table 3.1. The People.

Insiders	Outsiders
White	Non-whites
Religious	Secular
Christian	Muslim and Other Non-Christians
"Traditional" Women	Feminists
Heterosexual	LGBTQ
Hardworking	Lazy
Live in American heartland	Coastal elites
Capitalist	Socialist

chapter, where we examine the factors that led the Republican Party, once the "Party of Lincoln," to become the institutional home for right-wing populists.

The final point about defining "the people" as capitalists or capitalist cheerleaders points to the fact that business elites are not cast as the enemies of the people, while political and intellectual elites are. One factor at play here is that radical right-wing populists are disproportionately represented by small business owners, who identify with business elites. Part of the attractiveness of Trump is predicated on a more general idea that business acumen ought to be transferred to the political realm, and that political elites therefore ought to be replaced by business outsiders. The Republican Party has historically been seen as the party of business. However, a decisive ideological transformation took hold during the Reagan presidency, when neo-liberalism — an ideology committed to the proposition that markets should replace the state, that the political should be reduced to the logic of the economy — took hold (Block & Somers, 2014). Either unaware of the narrative that has questioned Trump's track record as a businessman or ignoring it, he was viewed by those embracing neo-liberalism as someone who would, as businesspersons presumably do, hire "the best and the brightest" and replace bureaucrats with those imbued with the entrepreneurial spirit. To maintain such an unquestioning faith in business elites, of course, requires ignoring their responsibility for the Great Recession of 2008 and the attendant suffering it caused.

CHAPTER 4

INSTITUTIONAL OPENINGS TO AUTHORITARIANISM

In an op-ed article that appeared in *The New York Times* 10 days after the election, Harvard politics professors Steven Levitsky and Daniel Ziblatt asked the question, "Is Our Democracy in Danger?" Turning to the work of the eminent political scientist Juan Linz, they pointed to three indicators of the rise of anti-democratic politicians: "a failure to reject violence unambiguously, a readiness to curtail rivals' civil liberties, and the denial of the legitimacy of elected government." Pointing to Trump's encouragement of violence at rallies, his threats to jail Hillary Clinton, and his repeated claims that the electoral process was rigged against him, they concluded that he — a "serial norm breaker" — constitutes an extremist authoritarian threat to democracy. There has been a widely held assumption that various "institutional filters" were in place to insure that such candidates would be prevented from winning the nomination of a major political party, let alone being elected — Levitsky and Ziblatt identifying the political party system and the news media as two vital filters. The filters failed in 2016, leading the authors to ponder what the future portends. Their measured conclusion is that although "American democracy is not in imminent danger of collapse" it is nevertheless true that "the warning signs are real."

This chapter examines the role that those two institutional filters played in 2016, looking first at the media and then at the Republican Party as it has developed into a party of the radical right since the 1960s. But before doing so, it is worth placing that discussion into a somewhat broader historical context. In *Democracy Index 2016: The Revenge of the "Deplorables"* the annual report on the state of democracy around the world produced by the Economist Intelligence Unit (part of the Economist Group that includes *The Economist*), the status of democracy in the United States was downgraded from a full democracy to a flawed one. Countries are ranked and located in one of four categories: full democracies, flawed democracies, hybrid regimes, and authoritarian regimes. The index is based on five factors: electoral process and pluralism, the functioning of government, political participation, political culture, and civil liberties. The nation's overall score fell to 7.98 in the most recent ranking. This is a significant decline over the course of a decade, for in 2006 the score was 8.22. By dropping below 8.0, it entered the ranks of flawed democracies, along with five other wealthy nations: Japan, Italy, France, Portugal, and Belgium. Comparing the US ranking to that of Canada is instructive. Whereas Canada, with a score of 9.15, is tied for sixth place and thus located in the list of full democracies, the United States is tied with Italy for 21st place. When compared to its neighbor, Canada scores higher on all five factors.

The report's authors concluded that the reason for the downgrade in status is a "trust deficit," a declining lack of confidence in the ability of political institutions to function, which is related to declining levels of political participation by the electorate. They observe that this decline precedes the 2016 election, and thus Trump was not the cause, but rather benefitted from it. They don't mention that since Reagan's mantra about government being the problem and not the solution, launching the era of neo-liberal ideology, the country has experienced a concerted effort by the right to call into question a role for government in providing for the social welfare of citizens. Neo-liberalism has led ever since to demands to reduce or eliminate existing programs while pushing privatization schemes designed to roll back a role for governmental agencies, using taxpayer dollars to fill the coffers of for-profit firms. In describing events that have led up to "this decline in popular confidence in public institutions" they include "the Vietnam War, the Watergate scandal, the Iraq wars, the financial crisis in 2008–2009, and repeated government shutdowns." It is worth noting that except for the Vietnam War, which involved both Democratic and Republican administrations, Republicans were in the driver's seat when the other three delegitimizing events occurred.

In addition, the analysts point to the role that income inequality has played, noting that "inequality is higher in the US than in other rich countries, and it has worsened since the financial crisis." The report leaves open the possibility of competing evaluations about what this portends. A pessimistic assessment might conclude that German social theorist Jürgen Habermas' account four decades earlier of the potential for a legitimation crisis to afflict advanced capitalist societies has today been realized and is very deep, posing an existential threat to pluralistic democracy. For the more optimistic, a considerably less foreboding assessment can be found in Stanford sociologist Larry Diamond's analysis of what he describes as "a global democratic recession." While the return to or intensification of authoritarianism is on the rise in many less democratically developed nations, in his view, the United States remains at the moment in a "modest recession of democracy" — one that needs to and can be contained by citizens committed to democratic "values and aspirations" before it "spirals into a depression." Diamond's prognosis, it is important to point out, was made prior to Trump's nomination (Diamond, 2015, p. 154).

THE MASS MEDIA: CHANNELS OF INFORMATION AND DISINFORMATION

The idea of the press as an autonomous institution that scrutinizes governmental activities and serves the vital function of informing the citizenry dates to at least the late eighteenth century, with commentators frequently pointing to Edmund Burke's depiction of the press as the fourth estate. Prior to the middle of the twentieth century, the idea of journalism was tied to one specific form of dissemination: the newspaper. Newspapers were the central conduits for providing the news, but they also served as sources of entertainment and as vehicles for advancing politically partisan viewpoints. Over the course of time, journalism emerged as a full-fledged profession, with specific codes of ethics — which sociologist Jeffrey C. Alexander (2016, p. 2) summarizes as "transparency, independence, responsibility, balance, and accuracy" — and the establishment of credentials, often via training in university journalism schools.

In describing the relationship between journalism and democracy, Professor of Journalism Michael Schudson has identified six specific functions performed by journalists: (1) provide information vital for citizens to make informed political choices; (2) undertake investigative reporting, particularly as it pertains to governmental power; (3) analyze the news by using rational frameworks that make a complex society comprehensible; (4) promote social empathy in order to help people understand the worldviews of others; (5) provide a public forum that encourages constructive dialogue among people with differing viewpoints; and (6) mobilize citizens for particular programs. In performing these functions, journalism serves a vital role in sustaining and enhancing the democratic project (Schudson, 2008, p. 12).

This ideal sets a high normative bar for journalism, one that can easily lead to disappointment about how it plays out in the real world, where it is interspersed with the commercial demands of an industry. And in recent years, the state of print journalism's economic health has led to growing concern about the future of journalism, combined with the impact of nonprint venues, which increasingly includes social media. Alexander is correct in observing that the "economic vise" squeezing contemporary journalism is due in no small part to the "social effects of the cultural mantra 'information will be free'" rather than to technological transformation per se (2016, p. 6). Despite these challenges, journalists have remained devoted to professional standards, and at least the three major national newspapers — *The New York Times*, the *Washington Post*, and the *Wall Street Journal* — are at the moment economically stable. And they have done valuable work. Indeed, we know who Trump is as a person, a businessman, and a political figure due chiefly to the efforts of journalists. That being said, the *Wall Street Journal* is a special case because it is owned by Rupert Murdoch, who aggressively promoted Trump's candidacy in his tabloid *New York Post*, and who has personal entanglements with the Trump family that are potentially troubling for the future of journalistic coverage of Trump at his flagship broadsheet.

In doing the interpretive work necessary to understand the electorate, an aspect of the narrative that was widely, though not universally, embraced had it that the typical Trump voter — the angry, forgotten, or silent American — who had lost out economically had turned to Trump as a "blow-up the system" populist. In addition, such voters were repeatedly described as new entries into electoral politics — a claim often made by Trump on the campaign trail. These voters presumably were largely constituted by people who had lost their jobs due to deindustrialization. Yet, as the preceding chapter makes clear, Trump voters had on average higher incomes than the population at large. Given that they are an older population, they are disproportionately located in the ranks of the retired. And rather than being political novices, they are long-term veterans of politics on the right wing of the Republican Party (some of them claim Independent status because they locate their politics to the right of the Republican Party). In this regard, not only are they like the Tea Party activists from a few years ago, but in fact many Tea Party activists, once the movement declined or at least the label lost its drawing power, switched seamlessly to becoming Trump supporters, moving without apparently noticing from being staunch free trade proponents to embracing economic protectionism.

In a useful analysis of Pew data, Leigh University political science professor Anthony DiMaggio has concluded that Trump supporters did not identify as priority issues those that would reflect economic anxiety. He wrote that, "Support for Trump is not significantly associated with public concerns about 'improving the job situation' nationally, 'strengthening the nation's economy', 'dealing with global trade issues', 'reducing health care costs', 'dealing with the problems of poor and needy people', or 'improving the educational system'." He found, in contrast, that the strongest predictors of support included the following: "interest in 'dealing with gun policy', concern with 'strengthening the US military', concern that Muslims are 'anti-American', disinterest in 'dealing with climate change', and disinterest in 'dealing with the problems of poor and needy people'." Additional predictors of support for Trump included lowering the federal budget and concerns about crime, terrorist attacks, and immigration.

In short, this interpretive framework proved to be flawed insofar as it has tended to convolute or at least muddle the difference between those who voted for Trump from that much larger category of citizens who didn't show up at the polls — those sufficiently alienated from the American political system that they opted for exit rather than voice. Given that the downgrade of the nation from full to flawed democracy is in part due to low levels of citizen participation — including voting — it behooves journalists (and social scientists) to pay greater attention to this population, and to try to understand the reasons they give and the factors that contribute to their withdrawal from public life. This is not a criticism that implies a failure on the part of journalists to perform their professional duties, but rather a criticism that suggests a need to rethink their interpretive framework in order to better capture the motives and life circumstances of citizens across the political spectrum — both those engaged in and those disengaged from the electoral process.

However, there was another problem with framing that is indicative of a failure to serve the public interest. This was the effort to frame Trump as a normal politician (e.g., the waiting for Godot-like belief that at some point he would pivot to the center and transform himself into a conventional politician) despite the fact that journalists were only too aware of his degrading of a culture of civility and decency. Given that they were on display every day of the campaign, while nothing remotely comparable emanated from the

Clinton campaign, journalists can be faulted for treating both candidates in equally negative terms, thus setting up false equivalencies (Wemple, 2016). In addition, coverage of policy issues was exceedingly light — which played into Trump's hand given that Clinton, the policy wonk, presented herself as a candidate with concrete and detailed policy proposals while Trump offered nothing comparable (Patterson, 2016).

Despite these criticisms, good journalism continues to be produced in the face of current challenges to the profession. The bad news is that the consumers of quality journalism have increasingly turned away from newspapers to alternative platforms. According to findings of the Pew Research Center, only 20% of Americans report that they often receive the news from newspapers. This compares to 57% for television, 38% for social media, and 25% for radio (Mitchell, Gottfried, Barthels, & Shearer, 2016). Non-newspaper reading members of the public are less informed because they don't get into subjects with the same degree of depth as print readers. This is because for television and radio viewers, the news presented is, quite simply, less detailed. In the case of readers who do their reading solely online, research reveals that they do more skimming than readers do with print versions.

Far more troubling, journalism finds itself competing for attention with entertainment and with propaganda. Television and radio are primary platforms for entertainment, though they have historically sectioned off time for reporting the news, which usually amounts to a distillation of journalistic reports to fit time constraints. Less information is on offer than in a newspaper and in more concise form. In addition, as cultural critic Neil Postman pointed out over three decades ago in his classic 1985 book *Amusing Ourselves to Death*, in what he called the "age of show business," there has been an increasing bleed between the news and entertainment leading to what has become commonly referred to as infotainment, a format in which the news presenters often acquire celebrity or quasi-celebrity status. Ratings driven entertainment could take several forms, including that of the dueling pundits, often engaged in vitriolic debates rather than rational dialogue, seeking to generate plenty of heat but no light. A pioneer in the genre, John McLaughlin, died months before the 2016 election. The format for "The McLaughlin Group," which ran for 34 years, called for vitriolic posturing on the part of panelists, skewed to the political right, offering opinions both on topics they may have known something about and others that they didn't. This program proved to be the template for many programs to come.

Trump proved to be a ratings bonanza for television executives. CBS's CEO Les Moonves said in February 2016 that while Trump's candidacy "may not be good for America, it's damn good for CBS." He was responding to concerns about the willingness of television networks to provide Trump with an inordinate amount of free airtime. He admitted to treating Trump like a circus act, its entertainment value meaning that "the money's rolling in and this is fun" (Collins, 2016). What made this possible was that television had helped make Trump's a household name as the star of a reality program, even though it was a middling performer. What also made it possible was an abrogation of the obligations one would expect from a network that also considers itself to be a member of the fourth estate. CBS was not alone in this regard. The mainstream television networks' duty to separate the entertainment side of their industry from the journalistic side was undoubtedly made more complicated by the Trump candidacy, but this is not a novel situation for them, and it is one that will inevitably occur again.

But failing to separate entertainment from journalism is not the central issue for one other television network, the most successful of the cable networks: Fox News. Rather, Fox News is unlike any of its rivals of the airwaves insofar as it has been widely critiqued as existing not to serve the fourth estate, but rather as a propaganda tool of the Republican Party. It has established itself as a filter through which all potential candidates for high office in the party of necessity court network executives seeking their blessing. Until his departure from the network in the summer of 2016, forced out as a result of a flood of accusations that finally caught up with a serial sexual harasser, Roger Ailes was Fox News and Fox News was Roger Ailes. Indeed, for two decades since Rupert Murdoch founded Fox and hired Ailes to be its CEO, he ran the operation with a remarkable degree of independence from his boss, whose willingness to give him free rein was predicated on Ailes' capacity to generate revenues for the Murdoch media empire. According to journalist Tim Dickinson, writing in 2011, Ailes generated profits contributing to nearly one-fifth of the total for Murdoch operations. Moreover, he did so with a "bare-bones newsgathering operation — Fox News has one-third the staff and 30 fewer bureaus than CNN." In short, Ailes' primary focus was not on journalism.

As Gabriel Sherman's unauthorized 2014 biography makes clear, Ailes' career can best be described as that of a political operative, one who understood television and who learned that he could make or break careers and shape the political narrative via the medium. From his early work salvaging Richard Nixon's political career through his unrelenting attacks on Barack Obama, he proved adept, as Dickinson correctly observed, at selling one particular product: fear. He came to the business with a visceral politics predicated on deep resentments and paranoia, which translated into the creation of a network as theatrical production — at once a theater of cruelty and a ministry of misinformation.

The network consistently gives voice to what Eric Alterman appropriately calls "self-credentialed" experts. Given that selling fear today goes far if the objects of fear are Muslims, it is entirely unsurprising that one expert would falsely claim that some cities in Europe have been taken over by Muslims and "non-Muslims just simply don't go in" — in this instance the city being described by the expert was England's second largest, Birmingham. Another such commentator erroneously asserted that certain neighborhoods in Paris are under the rule of sharia law, and the police are afraid to enter them (Alterman, 2015).

Ailes was a master of spin and of projecting a coordinated message that the on-air personalities were expected to promote. Thus, in an attempt to derail Obama before he had officially entered the Presidential race in 2007, the Fox message was that he was a Marxist, a Muslim, a black nationalist, and a dangerous Saul Alinsky-inspired radical (Alinsky being, in fact, a progressive advocate of pragmatic political organizing, and not a wild-eyed radical). Fox would be the television vehicle for keeping alive the birther conspiracy. Whatever the issue, the message *du jour* could be repeated 24/7 for extended periods of time. Thus, the tragic deaths of the US ambassador and three other Americans in a 2012 attack in Benghazi, Libya, became an incessant preoccupation with Fox, promulgating conspiracy theories about then Secretary of State Clinton's alleged failures and subsequent efforts at a cover-up. In this case, the seamless relationship between Fox and right-wing Republicans was palpable, as a Congressional inquiry headed by right-wing Rep. Trey Gowdy extended over 20 months and cost taxpayers over $5 million. In the end, the witch-hunt turned up nothing untoward, but the spectacle did serve its purpose, which was to damage Clinton's candidacy.

In *How Propaganda Works*, Jason Stanley notes that the goal of the outright lies and factual distortions, which are often easily refuted, is to have the cumulative effect of changing the way people perceive the world. Authoritarian rulers rely on propaganda to create an alternative reality, a post-truth world in which ultimately the people come to view the leader as the only source of truth. As such, propaganda constitutes a threat to democracy, which requires multiple sources of information and fora within which differing assessments of information can be rationally adjudicated. Ailes, from the beginning of his career, sought to work viewers' emotions — particularly fear and anger — and thus to facilitate an alternative political universe. While Fox has proven to be the most valuable asset in the promotion of right-wing politics, it is not alone. Indeed, in that smaller viewer universe of radio listeners, right-wing radio programs at both the local and national levels have a longer history than Fox. The loudest voice in that broadcasting booth is Rush Limbaugh, whose bombast has a loyal fan base, as Madonna from Lake Charles attests.

The Trump campaign produced fault lines in the right, with some radio program hosts viewing Trump as not a real conservative and as a morally repugnant person. Others enthusiastically embraced him, setting off what journalist Robert Draper, writing in 2016, called a "civil war within the right-wing media." But prior to Trump this sector of the airwaves operated with a general consensus about the need to insistently challenge what they saw as liberal bias in the media. Conservative talk-show host Charles Sykes has offered the following insider assessment of the disturbing unintended consequences of relentlessly pursuing that objective:

> *For years, as a conservative radio talk show host, I played a role in that conditioning by hammering the mainstream media for its bias and double standards.*

But the price turned out to be far higher than I imagined. The cumulative effect of the attacks was to delegitimize those outlets and essentially destroy much of the right's immunity from false information. We thought we were creating a savvier, more skeptical audience. Instead, we opened the door for President Trump, who found an audience that could be easily misled. (Sykes, 2017, p. R4)

According to political scientist Markus Prior's analysis of political polarization and the media, the percentage of the public who watches cable news, specifically Fox, CNN, and MSNBC, ranges between 10% and 15% of the voting-age population, and in the case of Fox viewers the evidence indicates that they do not watch alternative outlets of information (Prior, 2013). In short, this segment of viewers operates in a bunkered world, exposed only to right-wing media venues for information. Widely cited empirical evidence supporting Sykes' concern that right-wing media failed to produce a savvier and more skeptical audience derives from Fairleigh Dickinson University's PublicMind Poll. Researchers concluded that in terms of knowledge of domestic issues, people who relied solely on Fox for information were less well informed than people who reported watching no media whatsoever (Cassino, Woolley, & Jenkins, 2012).

One example can serve to illustrate the implications of the misinformation machine of Fox and right-wing radio on shaping a worldview at odds with facts and the truth — flooding media outlets with what Trump spokesperson Kellyanne Conway has described as "alternative facts." The example is climate change. Climate change deniers, including those who contend that climate change is a hoax or a conspiracy propagated by scientists (or in Trump's take on it, by the Chinese), have used these media as a platform to hammer home their position. In the process, they have called into question the legitimacy of scientific elites. In a study released by the University of New Hampshire's Carsey School of Public Policy that examined attitudes about renewable energy and climate change, researchers concluded that "Trump voters stand apart." Indeed, whereas only 25% of Trump voters believe that climate change is occurring and that it is caused by humans, the figure jumps to 90% for Clinton voters. For every other category of voter or nonvoter, the results ranged between 68% and 99%. A similar divide is evident when questioned about whether renewable energy should have a higher priority on the national agenda, with only Trump voters registering a result below 50% (Hamilton, 2017).

In the 1990s, when her husband's administration was under attack by the right, Hillary Clinton contended that a "vast right-wing conspiracy" was determined to bring it down. Treated at the time as hyperbole, the evidence today supports political scientist Richard Meagher's conclusion that conservative media "are just one component in the broad political networks built over the past few decades. Conservative talk radio, print publications, television networks, and internet sites have numerous connections, both direct and indirect, with the think tanks, advocacy organizations, academic research centers, and foundations that develop and promote the right's policy agenda" (2012, p. 469). And in so doing, the right-wing media have, as sociologists Ronald Jacobs and Eleanor Townsley have written, moved "further away from the dominant practices of the journalistic field, turning themselves into clearly delineated partisan interpretive communities, in which the crafting of political narratives is moving beyond the control of the political party leaders" (2014, p. 240).

It is, of course, leaders of the Republican Party that they have in mind. One can only surmise what those leaders must think about an Oval Office in which Trump and Bannon shape policy. In a recent report, readers learned that Bannon admires Julius Evola, a little-known Italian proponent of an ultra-reactionary philosophy that took concrete form in his enthusiasm for Nazism and in his belief that fascism Mussolini-style didn't go far enough. Evola was a harsh critic of humanism, democracy, and equality, while promoting the idea of racial hierarchy with white people — whom he called Children of the Sun — at the top and calling for a return to monarchial rule. Moreover, Bannon and many of his Breitbart acolytes embrace Evola's conviction that, in the words of Professor Richard Drake, changing the system "was not a question of contesting and polemicizing, but of blowing everything up" (quoted in Horowitz, 2017, p. 17).

FROM THE PARTY OF LINCOLN TO THE PARTY OF THE WHITE BACKLASH

During the two decades after World War II the nation's two major political parties could be described as centrist, the Democrats staking out the center-left and the Republicans the center-right. Both were coalition parties, with part of the Democratic constituency consisting of labor unions, leftists who had moved toward the political center from the New Deal forward, and Southern conservatives — the Dixiecrats. Republicans were to large extent defined by their advocacy on behalf of big business and traditional main street conservatives. The Republican Party represented a large enough tent to attract fiscal conservatives, libertarians, and social liberals. It also attracted a core of right-wing radicals, during the 1950s associated in particular with the John Birch Society, a virulently anti-communist organization that operated with secret cells and abounding in conspiracy theories about communist penetration of the federal government and other institutions.

One of the founding members of the Society was Fred Koch, the founder of Koch Industries and the father of Charles and David. Party leaders saw these extremists as a threat to conservatism, and undertook campaigns to contain rather than encourage them. Efforts were made, for example by William F. Buckley, to keep the Society's members in particular and the extremist right in general out of influential roles in the party. However, over the course of several decades, as the success of the brothers Koch attests, the radical right has succeeded in reshaping the party and moving it far from its nineteenth-century roots. The turning point in the party's remake began in the wake of the tumultuous 1960s — an era in which the combined impact of the civil rights movement, growing opposition to the Vietnam War, and the counterculture set the stage for what has played out for over a half century later. As Jane Mayer has chronicled in *Dark Money: The Hidden History of the Billionaires behind the Rise of the Radical Right* on the funding sources of the radical right, the Koch brothers are an important component of a much larger group of donors, including prominent family names like Bradley, Olin, and Scaife. Their collective attempt to reshape American conservatism into something considerably more reactionary was immeasurably aided by *Citizens United*, the 2010 Supreme Court decision opening the floodgates for "dark money" campaign funding.

The Southern Strategy and White Nationalism

As an indication that the GOP could justly claim the mantle of being the Party of Lincoln into the early 1960s, an examination of who supported two legislative landmarks of the civil rights movement, the Civil Rights Act of 1964 and the Voting Rights Act of 1965, is instructive. Democrats controlled both houses of Congress and the legislation was pushed by Democratic President Lyndon B. Johnson. But both bills passed with bipartisan support. In both legislative chambers for both bills, the Republican Party garnered a larger percentage of its members supporting the legislation than their Democratic counterparts. Thus, for the Civil Rights Act, 82% of Republican Senators and 76% of House members voted for the bill compared, respectively, to 71% in the Senate and 60% in the House for Democrats. Similarly, when the Voting Rights Act was passed the following year, 94% of Republican Senators and 80% of House members voted in favor of the bill, with 70% of Democratic Senators and 75% of the party's House members joining them. Moreover, as Todd Purdum's history of the Civil Rights Act points out, many Congressional Republicans played crucial roles, not only in actively working to pass this legislation, but in pushing for civil rights in several other legislative initiatives during the preceding decade (Purdum, 2014a).

The lower figures for Democrats — though still sizeable majorities — were a consequence of the Dixiecrat faction in the party. This can be seen when turning to another piece of landmark legislation passed in the same year as the Voting Rights Act, the Social Security Amendments Act which laid the foundations for federal insurance for the elderly under the Medicare program and for the poor under the provisions of the Medicaid program. Conservative southern Democrats had been part of the New Deal coalition during the 1930s, seeing programs such as Social Security as beneficial to their white constituents. Meanwhile, the business-dominated Republican party operated with hostility to anything it perceived to be creeping socialism, something from their perspective that was present in New Deal legislation and in President

Johnson's efforts to build on that legacy by expanding the welfare state via his Great Society initiatives. Unlike the bipartisan support for the previous two bills, this act was passed despite the opposition of Republicans. In the Senate, whereas 84% of Democrats voted for the bill, only 41% of their Republican counterparts did. Likewise, in the House, 81% of Democrats supported the legislation, compared to only 50% of Republicans.

Despite Republican support for the Civil Rights and Voting Rights Acts, Johnson saw the writing on the wall: the Democratic coalition was about to unravel as the South, a once solidly Democratic region, was about to exit the party. Bill Moyers, then an aide to Johnson, reported that the President told him, "I think we just delivered the South to the Republican Party for a very long time to come" (Moyers, 2004, p. 167). Indeed, it would not be long before powerful Congressional Southerners such as Strom Thurmond and Jesse Helms switched party allegiances, setting off a stampede of Democratic defections. For its part, the Republican Party opened its arms, with Richard Nixon implementing his "Southern strategy." In researching a biography of Nixon, John A. Farrell discovered a document in which Nixon, during the 1968 presidential campaign, promised these new arrivals to the party that he "would retreat on civil rights and 'lay off pro-Negro crap' if elected" (2017, p. 9). At the same time, liberal and moderate Republicans elsewhere in the country were confronted with challenges from the right by opponents who were hostile to their centrism and their commitment to civil rights. Thus began what Purdum describes as "the long process by which the Party of Lincoln became the party of white backlash, especially [but not only] in the South" (2014b, p. 3).

Writing in 1970, then Republican strategist Kevin Phillips contended in his case for the "emerging Republican majority" that as blacks who had achieved the franchise thanks to the Voting Rights Act flocked to the Democratic Party, so the movement of Southern whites into the Republican camp would accelerate. He also predicted that as blacks continued to migrate to Northern states, while Northern whites migrated southward, the impact of black voters remaining in the region in determining the outcomes of presidential elections would be limited. The end result, he predicted, would be that a once solidly Democratic South would become a solidly Republican region.

Nixon, of course, was elected twice, his administration ending in the self-inflicted failure of the Watergate scandal, in retrospect a not surprising end to the career of one who was so accomplished in the dark arts of politics. The 1970s set the stage for the final destruction of a center-right conservative party and the solidification of a reactionary one — a party in which people associated with the former were increasingly condemned by those in the latter camp as being Republicans in Name Only (Kabaservice, 2012).

The rise of Ronald Reagan to national prominence and his victory over the one-term President Jimmy Carter in 1980 further signaled this rightward shift. Thus, Reagan launched his 1980 post-convention campaign in Philadelphia, Mississippi, the site of the brutal murder of three civil rights workers in 1964. Far from being there to memorialize their martyrdom, he was there to inform whites that he was on their side, using the coded language of states' rights. The person who arranged this visit was Republican operative Paul Manafort, who would serve the Trump campaign until his Russian connections made it too problematic for him to continue in that role. His place in Republican politics from Reagan to Trump reflects a white nativism that has, arguably, defined the party ever since the implementation of the Southern strategy. It led to recurrently stoking racial fears and antagonisms, as with Lee Atwater's Willie Horton (a convicted murderer who went on a crime spree while on furlough) television advertisements on behalf of his boss, George H. W. Bush.

The Christian Right

Reagan had inherited a base of supporters who in the 1960s rallied around their doomed candidate Barry Goldwater, but Reagan's electoral victory would not have been possible had it not been for the alliance forged between the Republican Party and the Christian right. The latter was the term widely used during the 1980s to describe a religious social movement, while today the operative term in both self-presentation and in most media coverage is evangelical. The former carries with it a more overtly political dimension and a specific historical context, while the latter is a fuzzier term. For that reason, I prefer the term fundamentalist in characterizing movement leaders and organizations. It can be a term of disparagement, but in fact has greater analytic rigor, thus making it a more serviceable tool for analyzing this segment of American Christianity.

While all of the world's major religions contain fundamentalist elements or currents, the origins of the term are decidedly American, the outgrowth of a project funded by Southern Californian oil millionaire Lyman Steward to define the fundamentals of the Christian faith (including the inerrancy of the Bible, miracles, and the literalness of the resurrection) and to identify its enemies, which were many. They included socialism, feminism, Darwinism, Roman Catholicism, Mormonism, modern spiritualism, humanistic psychology, the Social Gospel, and theological liberalism. Those attracted to fundamentalism were prepared to press their religious worldview into the political realm, as they did in pressing Tennessee to pass a prohibition on the teaching of evolution in public schools, leading to one of the signature early moments in the cultural war between fundamentalists and their modernist opponents, the Scopes trial in 1925.

Historian Martin Marty, who led a major American Academy of Arts and Sciences project on fundamentalism, offered a succinct account of what fundamentalism is and what it is not. It is not, he argued, "the same thing as conservatism, traditionalism, classicism, or orthodoxy, though fundamentalists associate themselves with such concepts." They are "seldom opposed to technology" and in fact were quick to the game in exploiting the potential first of radio and then of television in promulgating their message. And they "are not always poor, uneducated people" as deprivation theories would have it. In fact, it is clear that many contemporary fundamentalists have entered into the middle class (Marty, 1988, pp. 17–19).

In identifying the core components of fundamentalism, Marty begins by stating that it "is always reactive, reactionary," forever responding to "perceived challenges and threats" posed by a "force, tendency, or enemy" that is "eroding, corroding, or endangering one's movement and what it holds dear." As such, fundamentalism is about defining boundaries, and defining them in bright, not blurred, terms: the world is us against them, with them being a sometimes shifting target. This means, Marty continues, that fundamentalism "is always an exclusive or separatist movement" predicated on beliefs that are defined in absolutist, black-and-white terms. It is for that reason that fundamentalists are dismissive of interfaith or ecumenical understanding and dialogue, opting instead for an oppositional stance against anyone who does not share their worldview. Marty concludes that fundamentalists are inherently absolutist, and, "With absolutism comes authoritativeness or authoritarianism" (Marty, 1988, pp. 20–21).

Such authoritarian tendencies do not necessarily translate into political action, for fundamentalists can, and some do, react to the world, to use the language of sociologist Martin Riesebrodt by fleeing it, effecting a symbolic and communal separation from it. However, when fundamentalists do opt to engage the world as a social movement, they seek to master it by imposing their beliefs and practices on it. It is precisely this category that many sociologists of religion call evangelical, leaving the term fundamentalist to account for the former category of believers (e.g., Christian Smith's 1998 work), but Riesebrodt's language of world mastering fundamentalists better captures the political aspirations of right-wing Christians. The strain of world mastering fundamentalists engaging in American politics since the middle of the past century includes such now largely forgotten figures as Carl McIntyre, a dissident Presbyterian and fervent anti-communist crusader — engaged as he saw it in a civilization struggle between the Christian West and the atheistic core of Soviet communism. He was hostile to anyone seen as fellow travelers, which included groups such as the ecumenically oriented National Council of Churches, making his views known to a radio audience via his "The 20th Century Reformation Hour." He and like-minded fundamentalists represent the precursors to the contemporary Christian right.

Movement mobilization took off in the 1970s. The movement took organizational form, as signified by the examples of two influential leaders, Pat Robertson and Jerry Falwell. Both were from Baptist backgrounds, but Robertson inflected his own religious practice with a charismatic flavor, thus bringing Pentecostalism into his operation. He founded the Christian Broadcast Network and hosts the "700 Club" program that was a regular network feature. He also created

Regent University and the American Center for Law and Justice, which aimed to shaped legislative agendas and fight judicial battles. For his part, Falwell — the pastor at the Thomas Road Baptist Church in Lynchburg, Virginia — also was a televangelist and as with Robertson got into higher education, founding Liberty University in 1971. He was also the founder and head of the Moral Majority, which he launched in 1979.

Many of the issues that have mobilized the movement's base have been consistent over time, none more-so than the four-plus decade effort to roll back the Supreme Court's 1973 *Roe v. Wade* decision legalizing abortion. Leaders have challenged separation of church and state by pressing for prayer in public schools and by promoting various strands of values education, such as abstinence-only sex education programs. Underpinning all of the particular issues preoccupying the Christian right is the conviction that the United States is a Christian nation and that, as the name of Falwell's organization indicates, the movement represents the beliefs of a majority of the citizenry. At the same time, the Christian right sees itself as under assault from enemies who threaten the cultural integrity of the nation. If the Southern strategy pushed the Republican Party into the camp of white nationalists, the Christian right's self-understanding is shaped by an ideology of Christian nationalism.

Sociologist of religion Rhys Williams has analyzed the boundary-defining work effected by Christian right leaders, writing that their self-identified enemies include "liberals, Hollywood, the media, the American Civil Liberties Union, and often, academics." He goes on to observe that what these secular elites are accused of sharing in common is "that they are hostile to religion and they are antipopulist. Both qualities show them to be fundamentally un-American." In making such accusations, these world mastering fundamentalists reveal their anti-pluralist and thus intrinsically anti-democratic view of politics (Williams, 2009, pp. 158–159). Williams's argument about the deep antipathy world mastering fundamentalists express toward secular elites has been confirmed in two studies conducted by researchers at the University of Minnesota over a 10-year period. In nationally representative samples, the researchers concluded that the great "Other" is the atheist. Two differences between their findings from 2004 compared to 2014 are first, that in 2014 those who describe themselves as spiritual but not religious are also looked upon with suspicion, and second, that Muslims are increasingly seen as not sharing "my vision of American society" (Edgell, Gerteis, & Hartmann, 2006; Edgell, Hartmann, Stewart, & Gerteis, 2016). The current animus toward Muslims reflects a long history of hostility to other religions, including anti-Semitism, anti-Catholicism, and anti-Mormonism. How much antipathy is directed to most other religions is today difficult to determine given that the spotlight is shining brightly on Islam.

Such is the boundary drawing required to make the claim to being a Christian nation. Bright boundaries do not permit consideration of the proposition that the United States is a Judeo-Christian nation, and certainly not that the Abrahamic religions are equally legitimate under the American sacred canopy. The assertiveness — indeed, the militancy — of the insistence on defining America as a Christian nation belies fear that it either no longer actually is or soon may no longer be so. This perspective is on display, for example, in Republican politician Mike Huckabee's 2015 book, *God, Guns, Grits, and Gravy*, which bemoans the growing secularization of the nation and the gulf between people of the heartland and liberal elites: the significant linkage in his book's title involves God and guns, and it is also worth noting that

Huckabee was also a program host at the Fox Network for several years.

The world according to Huckabee is also the world according to the National Rifle Association (NRA). The organization was founded shortly after the Civil War in response to the realization by Union officers that their soldiers were terrible marksmen. From that beginning, it developed into an organization devoted to hunting and sports shooting, and defined as part of its purpose to promote gun safety. It was not opposed in principal to gun laws, and thus supported bans on machine guns and sawed-off shotguns under the provisions of the National Firearms Act of 1934. By the 1960s a shift was underway to redefine guns in terms that evoked racial tensions, fear of crime, and other perceived threats to life and limb. Guns were portrayed as essential for law-abiding citizens to protect themselves, and thus any attempt to limit access to weapons was condemned. Michael Waldman, President of the Brennan Center for Justice at New York University and former Director of Speechwriting in Bill Clinton's administration, in an article on the rise of the NRA, quotes from an article that appeared in *Guns & Ammo* magazine that claimed that gun control advocates were "criminal-coddling do-gooders, borderline psychotics, as well as Communists and leftists who want to lead us into the one-world welfare state."

The person who led a coup that ousted the old NRA leaders at a contentious convention in Cincinnati in 1977 was Harlon Carter. Once he was elected executive vice-president of the organization, it was transformed into one that would oppose any gun control measures. Its absolutism riveted on an embrace of the Second Amendment, which had not loomed large in the NRA prior to this hostile takeover. As Waldman points out, "The NRA's lurch to the right was part of an abrupt shift across the Republican coalition." Wayne

LaPierre, who took over the role once held by Carter, pushed the NRA even further rightward, its work lobbying to prevent any gun control legislation seamlessly merged with its becoming, in effect, a lobbying arm of the gun industry. And it has been successful, as meaningful gun reform has been stymied since 1996 despite the rash of mass killings that succeed in temporarily — but only temporarily — capturing the nation's attention (Yanker, 2014).

The demographics of both gun ownership and opinions about gun control reveal a stark divide. More than twice as many whites own guns compared to blacks. Likewise, Republicans and conservatives by more than a 2:1 ratio are gun owners compared to Democrats and liberals (Morin, 2014). Furthermore, survey data collected in 2012 found that sizeable majorities of African American Protestants, Catholics, the religiously unaffiliated, and mainline Protestants favored the passage of stricter gun control laws, but only 38% of what the study identified as white evangelical Protestants agreed. Moreover, the more likely respondents were to describe themselves as a "pro-life" Protestant, the less inclined they were to support gun control legislation (PRRI, 2013; see also, Cox & Jones, 2012). They do so despite the fact that, as David Hemenway, Professor of Health Policy at Harvard, has made clear, there is a scientific consensus that "strong gun laws reduced homicide rates" (Hemenway, 2015). And they do so despite the fact, reported by the Centers for Disease Control, that more than 60% of gun-related deaths — approximately 20,000 per year — are suicides (Desilver, 2013).

Why do so many members of the Christian right believe that guns save lives? For the same reason that they believe that the crime rate has been rapidly escalating during the past quarter of a century, when the opposite is true. For the same reason that they are convinced that immigrants are entering the country in unprecedented numbers, in the process of taking American jobs, further increasing the crime rate, and undermining the national culture. For the same reason that they think Islam is not a religion, but rather a radical political movement intent on destroying western civilization. The reason is fear, the flames of which have been fanned by white nationalism and Christian nationalism, thus pushing its adherents ever further toward the extremist right. To comprehend this from the other side of the Protestant divide, one can turn to Pulitzer Prize winning novelist and essayist Marilynne Robinson, perhaps the most astute apologist of liberal Protestantism. She argues, "fear is not a Christian habit of mind," going on to contend that "it is potentially a very costly indulgence to fear indiscriminately, and to try to stimulate fear in others." Thus, pointing to reports of a growing number of Kalashnikovs being purchased in the country, she notes that during the Cold War the fear was that these weapons would be used in a "land war between great powers, that is, that they would kill Americans. Now, since they are being brought into this country, the odds are great that they will indeed kill Americans. But only those scary ones who want to destroy all we hold dear. Or, more likely, assorted adolescents in a classroom or a movie theater" (Robinson, 2015, pp. 125–130).

Trump's connection to the religious right needs to be understood by the juxtaposition of two facts: he is religiously illiterate and he needed to pander to this segment of the Republican base in order to win both the nomination and the election. Regarding the former, his limited acquaintance with Christianity was at the hands of Norman Vincent Peale, whose "power of positive thinking" amounted to what his biographer Christopher Lane calls "religio-psychiatry," a vacuous amalgam that was hooked on to a version of Christian nationalism. Peale was roundly criticized by theologians such as Reinhold Niebuhr and by the psychiatric profession. In terms of his politics, he was an opponent of the New Deal welfare state and his strident anti-Catholicism led him to depict the candidacy of John Kennedy as a threat to the nation.

Regarding the latter, it is not surprising that a mutual attraction developed between Trump and various big names associated with the prosperity gospel such as Detroit mega-church pastor Wayne T. Jackson and Florida-based Paula White and latter-day incarnations of the power of positive thinking such as Joel Osteen. First, all of these religious entre-preneurs share Trump's salesmanship directed at an audience they know how to impress, and his embrace of a luxury life-style. Second, at the level of their respective business ventures, the parallel between their organizations and the Trump Organization is striking. And, for that matter, for the more overtly political leaders of the contemporary Christian right, there is another parallel worth noting. Just as Trump's closely held and opaque family business is intergenerational, with the fourth generation being groomed to take over, so too are several of the prominent Christian right organizations lucra-tive family operations passed from father to son — from Pat to Gordon Robertson, from Jerry to Jerry Falwell, Jr., and from Billy to Franklin Graham.

Falwell endorsed Trump early on in the campaign, and in so doing indicated that fealty to the religious right from one of their own was not of paramount importance, lending a body blow to the candidacy of Ted Cruz. For his part, Franklin Graham said that he sensed the hand of God at work in electing Trump. In making their case, they had to contend with the fact that Trump was not one of them. Some religious right leaders were content to believe that God works in mysterious ways and sometimes uses nonbelievers to advance the faith. Others boldly asserted their conviction that

Trump was, in fact, a good Christian. James Dobson, the founder of Focus on the Family, an advocacy organization for conservative social values, was clearly aware of Trump's awkwardness with discussing sin and redemption, which prompted Dobson to characterize the 70-year old as a "baby Christian." For his part, Falwell said that Trump "lives a life of loving and helping others as Jesus taught in the Great Commandment" (Zylstra, 2016).

Obama as a Double Threat to the Tea Party

The 2008 historic election of Barack Obama set in motion a reaction that was intense, uncivil, and unrelenting. Republican Representative Joe Wilson upended congressional decorum by shouting that Obama was a liar while the President was giving a speech to a joint session of Congress. The Republican leader in the Senate quickly promised that the one objective of Senate Republicans would be to insure that Obama would not be re-elected, and to that end rejected bipartisanship at every turn. The right-wing media savaged him relentlessly, the Southern Poverty Law Center reported disturbing increases in the size and activities of right-wing hate groups, and funds from right-wing plutocrats flowed freely to mobilize the grassroots.

Obama had been exceedingly careful — too careful for many of his supporters' tastes — in addressing issues about race. Moreover, he had to simultaneously confront two crises, the first being the blowback caused by the disastrous Bush/Cheney invasion of Iraq and the second being the global financial crisis that began in 2007. Much of his agenda reflected both the need to respond carefully to these inherited problems, but beyond that he pressed what was essentially a pragmatic center-left set of proposals. His one major ambitious plan called for building on the New Deal and Great Society programs in addressing the fact that the United States was the only wealthy liberal democracy in the world that did not treat health care as a universal entitlement. He sought to expand health care coverage, reduce costs, and implement best practices that would make for a more efficient and effective health delivery system. And in so doing, rather than pressing for a single-payer system akin to Canada's or expanding Medicare to cover all Americans, he hoped for a plan that would elicit bipartisan support. To that end, the plan he proposed bore a family resemblance to one developed by a conservative think tank in the 1990s and a plan that Mitt Romney created in Massachusetts during his tenure as governor. Obstructionism would make bipartisanship impossible, and thus the Affordable Care Act was passed without a single Republican vote in either chamber of Congress.

In this context, the Tea Party came to represent the crystallization of citizen opposition to Obama. The intensity of their vehement hostility to Obama can be understood by the fact that as right-wing populists, their enemies were twofold: elites — governmental and academic, but not business — and the congeries of "Others," including blacks, immigrants, Muslims, and freeloaders. For them, Obama signified, was the very embodiment of, both enemies. He was the black usurper, his white mother in the end being irrelevant to this particular trope. He was the noncitizen, born in Kenya. He was the closet Muslim. At the same time, the Harvard Law graduate and part-time professor at the University of Chicago was a member of the elite liberal intelligentsia. Those who identified as strong Tea Party supporters, amounting to perhaps one-fifth of the electorate, were vocally unwilling to see Obama as a legitimate President.

Much discussion ensued about the precise character of the Tea Party. Was it a genuine grassroots movement or was it of the Astroturf variety, the product of the Koch brothers and other right-wing plutocrats? In *The Tea Party and the Remaking of Republican Conservatism* sociologists Theda Skocpol and Vanessa Williamson see it as both, observing that "one of the most important consequences of the widespread Tea Party agitations unleashed from the start of Obama's presidency was the populist boost given to professionally run and opulently funded right-wing advocacy organizations devoted to pushing ultra-free-market policies." These include FreedomWorks, the Club for Growth, the Tea Party Express, and Americans for Prosperity. The last of these is the creation of the Koch brothers, a nonprofit political advocacy organization. Its funders have spent millions pushing to privatize Social Security, voucherize Medicare and Medicaid, slash taxes, roll back environmental laws, and crush labor unions. For example, the organization shaped Governor Scott Walker's assault on public sector unions in Wisconsin and has been a central player in shaping Rep. Paul Ryan's agenda to roll back the welfare state. As oversight organizations promoting transparency have repeatedly pointed out, these operations are prime examples of the impact of dark money from wealthy right-wing donors who are able to keep their identities anonymous while spending freely to influence public policy.

Skocpol and Williamson succinctly summarize the purpose of these activities, writing that, "After the 2008 election, the Koch brothers and their organizational allies were determined to do all they could to limit, humiliate, and defeat Barack Obama and other Democrats in the US Congress and the states, majority democracy be damned." Along with right-wing think tanks such as the American Enterprise Institute, but particularly with the more extremist and strident Cato Institute and Heritage Foundation, these forces came to constitute the main drivers of Republican Party agendas. They also contributed heavily to congressional races, the result being the growing impact within the party of what is known today as the Freedom Caucus, composed of about 30 Republican House members. The defeat of Eric Cantor in Virginia by the even more right-wing David Brat was indicative of the rightward movement of the party.

Among the rank and file, activists often claimed that they were newcomers to the political process, outsiders who felt compelled by the clear and present danger the Obama presidency represented to get involved as patriots in defense of the nation. Such was not the case. In the main, these were long-term Republican Party members, their political views shaped by white nationalism, Christian nationalism, or by some combination thereof. In a 2011 report the Pew Research Center found that Tea Party members originate disproportionately from the ranks of white evangelical Protestants. On economic issues, they differ from the population as a whole by overwhelmingly preferring smaller government and by believing that corporate profits are fair and reasonable. On social issues, they differ from registered voters in general by opposing same-sex marriage and abortion at a higher level, while also being far more likely to oppose gun control. It is perhaps due to the religious backgrounds of so many Tea Party members, people who would claim to interpret the Bible literally as the inerrant word of God, that movement rhetoric about the Constitution was similarly reverential, treating it as a sacred text (Skocpol & Williamson, 2012, p. 48). And like Biblical literalists, they presumed to be able to interpret the Constitution in similar ways, dispensing with the ambiguities of language or a felt need to recognize the salience of historical context.

After Obama's reelection, the Tea Party looked to some observers to be a spent force. However, Skocpol, writing in 2013, correctly contended that it "wasn't going anywhere," and in fact maintained political influence at both the national and state levels. She concluded by making the following important point: "Americans may resent the Tea Party, but they are also losing ever more faith in the federal government — a big win for anti-government saboteurs. Popularity and 'responsible governance' are not the goals of Tea Party forces." In this regard, they clearly set the stage for Trump. Despite at one time being fierce advocates of limited government when confronted by what they described as a power-grabbing executive during the Obama years, they, ironically, were happy to support someone projecting himself as an autocratic strongman. Likewise, once proponents of a neo-liberal embrace of unfettered global capitalism found themselves equally enamored of economic protectionism during the 2016 campaign season. What didn't change was their visceral hostility to political enemies and to those who they had denied membership in the ranks of "the people." Writing in 2016, journalist Kate Aronoff correctly concluded that, "The infrastructure that paved Trump's road to electoral success was built largely by the Tea Party."

In a multiparty parliamentary system, right-wing populists would have created their own parties to compete in electoral politics — as has been going on in Western Europe for over three decades. In the US, context politics has long been dominated by two major parties, with third-party efforts never amounting to more than symbolic protests incapable of achieving actual political power. Thus, the triumph of right-wing populism required the takeover of the Republican Party. Whereas the extremist right had been successfully kept at arm length in the two decades after World War II, the Southern strategy and the entry of a politicized Christian right made the takeover possible. The deal was sealed when liberal and moderate Republicans either left or were forced out.

Right-wing populists are by now very much in control the party, running it, however, without widespread support among the electorate at large. How is this possible? Part of the reason has to do with the historically deeply entrenched electoral system that is, simply put, insufficiently democratic. Beyond that reality, Republican success at gerrymandering Congressional districts has created many safe seats for right-wing extremists. And a well-established part of the Republican playbook today is voter suppression. While the Voting Rights Act of 1965 made possible the exercise of the franchise by previously excluded minority groups, it has been met by a relentless campaign to make voting difficult or impossible. This campaign was greatly assisted by the victory of the conservative faction of the Supreme Court in 2013 to whittle away at the provisions of the law. And several states were quick to jump on this decision to enact laws that disproportionately and negatively impacted minority and poor voters. Finally, since the Reagan administration, the delegitimizing of government has contributed to the withdrawal from civic involvement, including voting, for a large plurality of the nation's adult citizens.

Many of the people in this group of disengaged citizens are the most economically vulnerable members of society, and Republican leaders know that if they voted with their own self-interest in mind, they would be unlikely to support a right-wing populist agenda. Thus, their success in achieving their reactionary goals is predicated in no small part on the ability to instill in these potential voters a sense of cynicism and fatalism. The electoral victory of Trump, who many on the right viewed as flawed but potentially useful, was made possible by these fundamental assaults on the democratic process and on the culture of democracy.

CHAPTER 5

POSTSCRIPT

Donald Trump is an unpopular President. In the immediate aftermath of American elections, both during the transition and in the earliest phase of a new administration, the electoral winner usually receives a bump in the public opinion polls — during what has long been called the "honeymoon" phase. The polling aggregation website FiveThirtyEight compared Trump's approval ratings to those of his predecessors going back to Harry Truman, tracing those ratings from inauguration day and in the case of past Presidents extending the graph for each of these administration's first 300 days. Only two Presidents began their terms with a less than 50% approval rating: George W. Bush, who entered office after a contested election involving the Supreme Court and after losing the popular vote by over a half million votes, and Donald Trump. Trump's 45% approval rating as his administration began was two percentage points lower than Bush's. And for comparative purposes, it contrasts to Barack Obama's 68% approval rating in 2009. Moreover, whereas Bush's approval ratings steadily climbed during the next few months of his administration, the trend line is in the opposite direction for

Trump, dropping several percentage points three-quarters of the way to his first 100 days in office.

His dyspeptic inaugural address was delivered to a crowd much smaller than Obama's 2009 inauguration, a fact that might not have become the subject of sustained discussion was it not for the fact that Trump and his Press Secretary Sean Spicer insisted otherwise — going so far as to challenge the National Park Service's estimates and dispute the visual evidence provided by their aerial and land photography from both inaugurations. High-profile resistance to the administration commenced the following day, with the Woman's March bringing a crowd to the capitol that experts informed reporters Tim Wallace and Alicia Parlapiano was three times larger than that attending the previous day's event. The adversarial nature of Spicer's first news briefing set the stage for a confrontational relationship with the media. Criticism of the press escalated in the first few weeks of the administration, culminating in a Presidential tweet in mid-February in which Trump declared that the press "is the enemy of the American people." Whether or not he understands the Stalinist lineage of the language, the statement elicited widespread condemnation, reflecting as it did a lack of appreciation of the critical role played by the fourth estate in democracies.

Governance has proven to be a challenge for Trump, who seeks to translate the way he ran a family-owned business to the governance of the world's largest democracy. Hundreds of appointments to key positions have yet to be filled, and thus questions are being raised about what this portends for the administration's ability to get things done. Two Executive Orders that were designed to fulfill his promise to implement a Muslim ban once in office have been stymied by the courts on constitutional grounds. As with the majority of Republicans in Congress, Trump had promised a quick repeal of the Affordable Care Act and its replacement by something he contended would be a vast improvement on a law that opponents contended was in a death spiral. Instead, on his 64th day in office, the bill that originated in the House under the leadership of Paul Ryan and received the full support of Trump was pulled shortly before a scheduled vote, once it was clear that its sponsors did not have the votes needed for passage. This was a bill that, according to the nonpartisan Congressional Budget Office, would have resulted in 24 million fewer people covered by health insurance — including a disproportionately large number of Trump voters.

This is not to suggest that nothing is being done, for Trump has signed a flurry of Executive Orders and several of his most extreme right-wing cabinet appointments have used their offices to take aim at such things as public schools, science funding, environmental regulation, climate change, and civil rights. From this perspective, it appears that the administration intends to pursue a hard-right agenda.

But it will do so under two clouds that may turn into a dark sky for the administration. The first concerns issues of corruption, an issue relevant not only to Trump, but extending to his family members and several prominent — and very wealthy — members of his cabinet. Even before the inauguration, ethics experts were questioning a wide range of troubling potential conflicts of interest. One, University of Minnesota law professor Richard Painter, who served as the chief ethics lawyer in George W. Bush's administration, has sued the President and has become a regular fixture on the airwaves pressing for attention to be paid to what he sees as multiple ethical improprieties and potential conflicts of interest. The second cloud concerns the role that Russia played in seeking to tilt the election to Trump, and whether there is evidence of collusion between Russian operatives and Trump associates. The headline of the March 20 edition of *The New York Times* announced that the "F.B.I. Is Investigating Trump's

Russia Ties, Comey Confirms" (Apuzzo, Rosenberg, & Huetteman, 2017). Where this is headed is at this point difficult to discern, but one thing appears clear: at this writing, 75 days after his inauguration, Trump is embroiled in controversies that have the potential to undermine his tenure in office. It must be disconcerting to his supporters to hear the following question, with the specter of Watergate behind it, being raised with increasing frequency: "What did the President know and when did he know it?"

Working the binaries did not end on Election Day, but rather continues in the current highly polarized political climate. In a poll conducted one month after Trump entered office, the Pew Research Center (2017) found that there was widespread disapproval of the way Trump was handling the job and similarly about specific policies. His overall disapproval rate of 56% was a record for a President at this stage of an administration (the previous low was Bill Clinton in 1993, with a 23% disapproval rating). The first initiative of the Trump administration was to issue an Executive Order stopping refugees from entering the country from seven majority-Muslim nations. This initiative did not reflect the views of a majority of respondents, with 59% expressing disapproval. Likewise, majorities disapproved of his handling of the threat of terrorism (53%), immigration policy (62%), and foreign policy (59%), while at 47% to 43% the public disapproved of his overall handling of the economy. These findings were reinforced in a poll released in early April by the Quinnipiac University Poll. Their findings on the issues examined by Pew were very similar. Quinnipiac also asked about what people thought about the way the administration was handling the environment; the disapproval level on this issue was 61%.

Compounding the disapproval of Trump's positions on these issues is the assessment of the public about his democratic leadership traits. On this front, it would appear that the impact of the anti-Trump narratives discussed in Chapter 2 are intensifying, winning out over the narrative that Trump's supporters would like to advance. Indeed, press reports indicate that there is growing consternation in the White House that they are losing control of the narrative. Pew's findings reveal that 57% of the public does not consider Trump to be well-informed, 59% do not believe he is trustworthy, 63% do not consider him to be a good communicator, and 68% disagree with the assertion that he is even-tempered. When asked if he will keep his business interests separate from his role as President, placing public service above self-interest, 58% do not believe that he will. And, suggesting the particular impact of the third narrative, that concerning Trump's political worldview, 59% of Americans say that he has little or no respect for the nation's democratic institutions. These findings were also reinforced in the Quinnipiac Poll: 61% of Americans think that he is not honest; 55% think he does not have good leadership skills; 57% do not think he cares about average Americans; 66% agree with the statement that he is not level-headed; and 61% do not think he shares their values. With these results, it is not surprising that the poll found that only 35% of Americans gave Trump a positive approval rating. The Republicans in Congress fared even worse, with an approval rating of only 21%. Finally, in a question one does not generally find in surveys of this sort, the pollsters asked if Trump as President made people proud or if the Trump presidency embarrassed them. 52% of Americans reported being embarrassed, while only 27% reported that they were proud (19% said they don't feel either).

Trump's improbable nomination to head a major political party and his even more improbable electoral victory was made possible by a sufficiently mobilized segment of the electorate harboring illiberal populist views antithetical to a democracy and the democratic culture that nourishes it. This segment included most significantly those representing the racialist backlash to the civil right movement and similar movements of other disadvantaged minorities, and conservative religious nationalists — both fundamentally hostile to pluralism. And when that same antipluralist and illiberal political worldview permeates one of those major political parties and is given voice in media outlets that serve as propaganda outlets for those voices — abrogating any pretense of being a genuine member of the fourth estate — what we confront are, as David Frum, the conservative senior editor at *The Atlantic* argues, "the preconditions for autocracy" (Frum, 2017, p. 49). The *modus operandi* of the would-be autocrat is a politics of cruelty, one that stokes fear, anxiety, resentment, arrogance, and stigmatization, and in so doing undermines values fundamental to democratic culture and the norms it nurtures — civility, mutuality, equality, respect, and a commitment to justice and the common good.

Frum is far from alone in believing that, "We are living through the most dangerous challenge to the free government of the United States that anyone alive has encountered" (Frum, 2017, p. 59). Indeed, American democracy's future is dim if too many of its citizens acquiesce into what the late Harvard political theorist Judith Shklar called "passive injustice," failing to act to bolster the cultural and institutional foundations of a democratic society. Fortunately, the signs of resistance are there, and the resistance has intensified. Rather than succumbing to the temptations of fear, cynicism, or complacency, there are hopeful signs of an increasingly resolute commitment by many citizens in the vital center who are intent to not simply salvage a flawed democracy but to strive to make it more democratic than it has ever been.

REFERENCES

Achen, C. H., & Bartels, L. M. (2016). *Democracy for realists: Why elections do not produce responsive government.* Princeton, NJ: Princeton University Press.

Adorno, T., Frenkel-Brunswik, E., Levinson, D., & Sanford, N. (1950). *The authoritarian personality.* New York, NY: Harper and Brothers.

Akkerman, A., Mudde, C., & Zaslove, A. (2014). How populist are the people? Measuring populist attitudes in voters. *Comparative Political Studies, 47*(9), 1324–1353.

Alexander, J. C. (2006). *The civil sphere.* New York, NY: Oxford University Press.

Alexander, J. C. (2010). *The performance of politics: Obama's victory and the democratic struggle for power.* New York, NY: Oxford University Press.

Alexander, J. C. (2016). Introduction: Journalism, democratic culture, and creative reconstruction. In J. C. Alexander, E. B. Breese, & M. Leungo (Eds.), *The crisis of journalism reconsidered: Democratic culture, professional codes, digital futures* (pp. 1–28). New York, NY: Cambridge University Press.

Alexander, J. C., & Jaworsky, B. N. (2014). *Obama power.* Cambridge: Polity Press.

Alford, H. (2015). Is Donald Trump actually a narcissist? *Vanity Fair,* November 11. Retrieved from http://www.vanity fair.com/news/2015/11/donald-trump-narcissism-therapists/. Accessed on December 7, 2016.

Alter, A. (2017). Uneasy about the future, readers turn to dystopian classics. *The New York Times,* January 27. Retrieved from https://www.nytimes.com/2017/01/27/business/media/dystopian-classics-1984-animal-farm-the-handmaids-tale.html. Accessed on April 4, 2017.

Alterman, E. (2015). Fox News: The world's comic relief. *The Nation,* January 28. Retrieved from https://www.thenation.com/article/fox-is-funny/. Accessed on February 3, 2017.

Apuzzo, M., Rosenberg, M., & Huetteman, E.. (2017). F.B.I. is investigating Trump's Russia ties, Comey confirms. *The New York Times,* March 20. Retrieved from https://www.nytimes.com/2017/03/20/us/politics/fbi-investigation-trump-russia-comey.html Accessed on April 5, 2017.

Aronoff, K. (2016). Trump and the Tea Party. *Jacobin,* March 26. Retrieved from https://www.jacobinmag.com/2016/03/tea-party-donald-trump-ted-cruz/. Accessed on February 15, 2017.

Austen, I. (2016). Trump tower in Toronto is in receivership after poor sales. *The New York Times,* November 4. Retrieved from http://www.nytimes.com/2016/11/05/world/americas/canada-trump-tower-toronto.html. Accessed on December 12, 2016.

Barthel, M., Mitchell, A., & Holcomb, J. (2016). *Many Americans believe fake news is sowing confusion.* December 15.

Retrieved from http://www.journalism.org/category/publications/. Accessed on December 16, 2016.

Blair, G. (2000). *The Trumps: Three generations that built an empire*. New York, NY: Simon and Schuster.

Block, F., & Somers, M. R. (2014). *The power of market fundamentalism: Karl Polanyi's critique*. Cambridge, MA: Harvard University Press.

Blow, C. (2016). Trump's age of idiocracy. *The New York Times*, December 5, p. A21.

Brooks, D. (2016). Donald Trump's sad, lonely life. *The New York Times*, October 11. Retrieved from http://www.nytimes.com/2016/10/11/opinion/donald-trumps-sad-lonely-life.html?_r=0. Accessed on December 5, 2016.

Bump, P. (2016). Bill O'Reilly rose to the defense of white privilege in America's presidential voting process. *The Washington Post*, December 21. Retrieved from https://www.washingtonpost.com/news/the-fix/wp/2016/12/21/bill-oreilly-rose-to-the-defense-of-white-privilege-in-americas-presidential-voting-process/?utm_term=.9c1397032fd4. Accessed on January 6, 2017.

Campbell, A., Converse, P., Miller, W., & Stokes, D. (1960). *The American voter*. New York, NY: John Wiley & Sons.

Cassidy, J. (2016). Trump University: It's worse than you think. *The New Yorker*, June 2. Retrieved from http://www.newyorker.com/news/john-cassidy/trump-university-its-worse-than-you-think. Accessed on December 13, 2016.

Cassino, D., Woolley, P., & Jenkins, K. (2012). *What you know depends on what you watch: Current events knowledge across popular news sources*. Fairleigh Dickinson University's

PublicMind Poll, May 3. Retrieved from http://publicmind. fdu.edu/2012/confirmed/. Accessed on February 3, 2017.

Collins, E. (2016). *Les Moonves: Trump is 'Damn Good for CBS'*. February 29. Retrieved from http://www.politico.com/ blogs/on-media/2016/02/les-moonves-trump-cbs-220001. Accessed on February 6, 2017.

Cox, D., & Jones, R. P. (2012). Slim majority of Americans support passing stricter gun control laws. *PRRI*, August 15. Retrieved from http://www.prri.org/research/august-2012-prri-rns-survey/#.VZG1-flVhBc. Accessed on February 13, 2017.

Cox, J. W. (2016). *Let's party like it's 1933: Inside the alt-right world of Richard Spencer*. November 22. Retrieved from https://www.washingtonpost.com/local/lets-party-like-its-1933-inside-the-disturbing-alt-right-world-of-richard-spencer/ 2016/11/22. Accessed on January 18, 2017.

Craig, S. (2016). Trump's empire: A maze of debts and opaque ties. *The New York Times*, August 20. Retrieved from http://www.nytimes.com/2016/08/21/us/politics/donald-trump-debt.html. Accessed on December 14, 2016.

Crain, C. (2016). None of the above: The case against democracy. *The New Yorker*, November 7, pp. 67–71.

Cramer, K. J. (2016). *The politics of resentment: Rural consciousness in Wisconsin and the rise of Scott Walker*. Chicago. IL: University of Chicago Press.

D'Antonio, M. (2016). *The truth about Trump*. New York, NY: Thomas Dunne Books.

Dahl, R. (1998). *On democracy*. New Haven, CT: Yale University Press.

Danner, M. (2016). The real Trump. *The New York Review of Books* (pp. 8–14), December 22, 2016.

Delli Carpini, M. X. (2005). An overview of the state of citizens' knowledge about politics. In M. S. McKinney, L. L. Kaid, D. G. Brystrom, & D. B. Carlin (Eds.), *Communicating politics: Engaging the public in democratic life* (pp. 27–40). New York, NY: Peter Lang.

Desilver, D. (2013). *Suicides account for most gun deaths*. Pew Research Center, May 24. Retrieved from http://www.pewresearch.org/fact-tank/2013/05/24/suicides-account-for-most-gun-deaths/. Accessed on February 14, 2017.

Desilver, D. (2016). *U.S. voter turnout trails most developed countries*. Pew Research Center, August 2. Retrieved from http://www.pewresearch.org/fact-tank/2016/08/02/u-s-voter-turnout-trails-most-developed-countries/. Accessed on January 6, 2017.

Diamond, L. (2015). Facing up to the democratic recession. *Journal of Democracy*, 26(1), 141–155.

Dickinson, T. (2011). How Roger Ailes built the Fox News fear factory. *Rolling Stone*, May 25. Retrieved from http://www.rollingstone.com/politics/news/how-roger-ailes-built-the-fox-news-fear-factory-20110525. Accessed on February 3, 2017.

DiMaggio, A. (2016). Donald Trump and the myth of economic populism: Demolishing a false narrative. *Counterpunch*, August 16. Retrieved from http://www.counterpunch.org/2016/08/16/donald-trump-and-the-myth-of-economic-populism-demolishing-a-false-narrative/. Accessed on February 15, 2017.

Draper, R. (2016). How Donald Trump's candidacy set off a civil war within the right-wing media. *The New York Times*, October 2, pp. 36–41, 54–55.

Eaglesham, J., Maremont, M., & Schwartz, L. (2016). How Donald Trump's web of LLCs obscures his business interests. *The Wall Street Journal*, December 8. Retrieved from http://www.wsj.com/articles/how-donald-trumps-web-of-llcs-obscures-his-business-interests-1481193002. Accessed on December 14, 2016.

Eberstadt, N. (2016). *Men without work: America's invisible crisis*. West Conshohocken, PA: Templeton Press.

Eco, U. (1995). Ur-Fascism. *The New York Review of Books*, June 22. Retrieved from http://www.nybooks.com/articles/1995/06/22/ur-fascism/?printpage=true. Accessed on August 10, 2016.

Edgell, P., Gerteis, J., & Hartmann, D. (2006). Atheists as 'Other': Moral boundaries and cultural membership in American society. *American Sociological Review*, 71(2), 211–234.

Edgell, P., Hartmann, D., Stewart, E., & Gerteis, J. (2016). Atheists and other cultural outsiders: Moral boundaries and the non-religious in the United States. *Social Forces*, 95(2), 607–638.

Eichenwald, K. (2016). Donald Trump's many business failures, explained. *Newsweek*, August 2. Retrieved from http://www.newsweek.com/2016/08/12/donald-trumps-business-failures-election-2016-486091.html. Accessed on December 12, 2016.

Fahrenthold, D. A. (2016a). Four months after fundraiser, Trump says he gave $1 million to veterans groups. *The*

Washington Post, May 24. Retrieved from https://www.
washingtonpost.com/news/post-politics/wp/2016/05/24/four-
months-later-donald-trump-says-he-gave-1-million-to-veterans-
group/?tid=a_inl&utm_term=.91901606ba1f. Accessed on
May 1, 2017.

Fahrenthold, D. A. (2016b). Trump boasts about his philan-
thropy, but his giving falls short of his words. *The
Washington Post*, October 29. Retrieved from https://www.
washingtonpost.com/politics/trump-boasts-of-his-philanthropy-
but-his-giving-falls-short-of-his-words/2016/10/29/b3c03106-
9ac7-11e6-a0ed-ab0774c1eaa5_story.html?utm_term=.
f218c371fc18. Accessed on December 13, 2016.

Fahrenthold, D., & Helderman, R. S. (2016). Trump bragged
that his money bought off politicians. Just not this time. *The
Washington Post*, September 7. Retrieved from https://www.
washingtonpost.com/politics/trump-bragged-that-his-money-
bought-off-politicians-just-not-this-time/2016/09/07/
00a9d1e4-750b-11e6-be4f-3f42f2e5a49e_story.html?utm_
term=.549a79dd45a3. Accessed on April 28, 2017.

Farhi, P. (2016). What really gets under Trump's skin? A
reporter questioning his net worth. *The Washington Post*,
March 8. Retrieved from https://www.washingtonpost.com/
lifestyle/style/that-time-trump-sued-over-the-size-of-hiswallet/
2016/03/08/785dee3e-e4c2-11e5-b0fd-073d5930a7b7_story.
html?utm_term=.3d178f363dcf. Accessed on December 13,
2016.

Farrell, J. A. (2017). Tricky Dick's Vietnam treachery. *The
New York Times*, January 1, p. 9.

Fishwick, C. (2016). Why did people vote for Donald
Trump? Voters explain. *The Guardian*, November 9.
Retrieved from https://www.theguardian.com/us-news/2016/

nov/09/why-did-people-vote-for-donald-trump-us-voters-explain. Accessed on January 13, 2017.

FiveThirtyEight. (2017). *How unpopular is Donald Trump?* April 5. Retrieved from https://projects.fivethirtyeight.com/trump-approval-ratings/. Accessed on April 5, 2017.

Flowers, A. (2016). *Where Trump got his edge.* November 11. Retrieved from http://fivethirtyeight.com/features/where-trump-got-his-edge/. Accessed on December 16, 2016.

Freedman, S. G. (2016). 'Church Militant' theology is put to new, and politicized, use. *The New York Times*, December 31, pp. A12–A13.

Frum, D. (2017). How to build an autocracy, *The Atlantic*, March, pp. 48–59.

Gerson, M. (2016). Trump reveals fragility at the heart of American democracy. *The Washington Post*, October 20. Retrieved from https://www.washingtonpost.com/opinions/trump-reveals-fragility-at-the-heart-of-american-democracy/2016/10/20/88651596-96d3-11e6-bc79-af1cd3d2984b_story.html?utm_term=.179b2bd162bf. Accessed on January 2, 2017.

Gilmore, M. (2012). Bob Dylan unleashed. *Rolling Stone*, September 27. Retrieved from http://www.rollingstone.com/music/news/bob-dylan-unleashed-a-wild-ride-on-his-new-lp-and-striking-back-at-critics-20120927. Accessed on January 20, 2017.

Goffman, E. (1963). *Stigma: Notes on the management of spoiled identity.* Englewood Cliffs, NJ: Prentice-Hall.

Gorski, P. (2017). *American covenant: A history of civil religion from the puritans to the present.* Princeton, NJ: Princeton University Press.

Gould, S., & Harrington, R. (2016). *7 charts show who propelled Trump to victory*. November 10. Retrieved from http://www.businessinsider.com/exit-polls-who-voted-for-trump-clinton-2016-11. Accessed on December 16, 2016.

Gramlich, J. (2016a). *Voters' perceptions of crime continue to conflict with reality*. November 16. Retrieved from http://www.pewresearch.org/fact-tank/2016/11/16/voters-perceptions-of-crime-continue-to-conflict-with-reality/. Accessed on December 16, 2016.

Gramlich, J. (2016b). *Most Americans haven't heard of the 'alt-right'*. December 12. Retrieved from http://www.pew research.org/fact-tank/2016/12/12/most-americans-havent-heard-of-the-alt-right/. Accessed on December 16, 2016.

Grey, S. (2016). Is Trump actually a 'fascist'? *The Establishment*, March 16. Retrieved from http://www.the-establishment.co/2016/03/16/is-trump-actually-a-fascist/. Accessed on December 15, 2016.

Gross, N. (2016). Are Americans experiencing collective trauma? *The New York Times*, December 16. Retrieved from http://www.nytimes.com/2016/12/16/opinion/sunday/are-americans-experiencing-collective-trauma.html?_r=0. Accessed on January 2, 2017.

Habermas, J. (1975). In T. McCarthy (Trans.). *Legitimation crisis*. Boston, MA: Beacon Press.

Hamilton, L. C. (2017). On renewable energy and climate, Trump voters stand apart. Carsey School of Public Policy, University of New Hampshire, National Issue Brief #113. Retrieved from http://scholars.unh.edu/cgi/viewcontent.cgi?article=1292&context=carsey. Accessed on February 7, 2017.

Hankes, K. (2017). *With questions of ideological 'purity tests', the alt-right stumbles.* January 11. Retrieved from https://www.splcenter.org/hatewatch. Accessed on January 18, 2017.

Harder, J., & Krosnick, J. A. (2008). Why do people vote? A psychological analysis of causes of voter turnout. *Journal of Social Issues, 64*(3), 525–549.

Helderman, R. (2016). Trump agrees to $25 million settlement in Trump University fraud cases. *The Washington Post*, November 18. Retrieved from https://www.washington post.com/politics/source-trump-nearing-settlement-in-trump-university-fraud-cases/2016/11/18/8dc047c0-ada0-11e6-a31b-4b6397e625d0_story.html?utm_term=.c74708b58e14. Accessed on December 13, 2016.

Hemenway, D. (2015). *There's scientific consensus on guns—and the NRA won't like it.* April 22. Retrieved from http://www.latimes.com/nation/la-oe-hemenway-guns-20150423-story.html. Accessed on February 14, 2017.

Herbst, S. (2010). *Rude democracy: Civility and incivility in American politics.* Philadelphia, PA: Temple University Press.

Hetherington, M. J., & Weiler, J. D. (2009). *Authoritarianism and polarization in American politics.* New York, NY: Cambridge University Press.

Hochschild, A. R. (2016). *Strangers in their own land: Anger and mourning on the American right.* New York, NY: The New Press.

Hochschild, J. L. (2010). If democracies need informed voters, how can they thrive while expanding enfranchisement? *Election Law Journal: Rules, Politics, and Policy, 9*(2), 111–123.

Hofstadter, R. (1964). The paranoid style in American politics. *Harper's Magazine*, November, pp. 77–86.

Holan, A. D. (2016). In context: Hillary Clinton and the 'Basket of Deplorables'. Retrieved from http://www.politifact.com/truth-o-meter/article/2016/sep/11/context-hillary-clinton-basket-deplorables/. Accessed on January 4, 2017.

Horowitz, J. (2017). Fascists too lax for a philosopher cited by Bannon. *The New York Times*, February 12, p. 17.

Huckabee, M. (2015). *God, guns, grits, and gravy*. New York, NY: St. Martin's Press.

Jacobs, R., & Townsley, E. (2014). The hermeneutics of Hannity: Format innovation in the space of opinion after September 11. *Cultural Sociology*, *8*(3), 240–257.

Johnston, D. C. (2016). *The making of Donald Trump*. Brooklyn, NY: Melville House.

Judis, J. B. (2016). *The populist explosion: How the great recession transformed American and European politics*. New York, NY: Columbia Global Reports.

Kabaservice, G. (2012). *Rule and ruin: The downfall of moderation and the destruction of the Republican Party, from Eisenhower to the Tea Party*. New York, NY: Oxford University Press.

Kagan, R. (2016a). There is something very wrong with Donald Trump. *The Washington Post*, August 1. Retrieved from https://www.washingtonpost.com/opinions/there-is-something-very-wrong-with-donald-trump/2016/08/01/. Accessed on December 4, 2016.

Kagan, R. (2016b). This is how fascism comes to America. *The Washington Post*, May 18. Retrieved from https://www.washingtonpost.com/opinions/this-is-how-fascism-comes-to-america/2016/05/17/c4e32c58-1c47-11e6-8c7b-6931e66333e7_story.html?utm_term=.5ca24c4795fb. Accessed on December 15, 2016.

Katznelson, I. (2005). *When affirmative action was white: An untold history of racial inequality in twentieth-century America*. New York, NY: W.W. Norton.

Kelkar, K. (2016). *Electoral college is 'Vestige' of slavery, say some constitutional scholars*. Retrieved from http://www.pbs.org/newshour/updates/electoral-college-slavery-constitution/. Accessed on January 5, 2017.

Kivisto, P., & Faist, T. (2007). *Citizenship: Discourse, theory, and transnational prospects*. Malden, MA: Blackwell Publishing.

Koerth-Baker, M.. (2016). Psychiatrists can't tell us what they think about trump. June 6. Retrieved from http://fivethirtyeight.com/features/psychiatrists-cant-tell-us-what-they-think-about-trump/. Accessed on December 5, 2016.

Kranish, M., & Fisher, M. (2016). *Trump revealed: An American journey of ambition, ego, money, and power*. New York, NY: Scribner.

Krauthammer, C. (2016). Donald Trump and the fitness threshold. *The Washington Post*, August 4. Retrieved from https://www.washingtonpost.com/opinions/donald-trump-and-the-fitness-threshold/2016/08/04/. Accessed on December 5, 2016.

Lane, C. (2016). *Surge of piety: Norman Vincent Peale and the remaking of American religious life*. New Haven, CT: Yale University Press.

Levitsky, S., & Ziblatt, D. (2016). Is our democracy in danger? *The New York Times*, December 18, p. SR 5.

Lewis, S. (1935). *It can't happen here*. New York, NY: Doubleday, Doran, and Co.

Lilla, M. (2016). The end of identity liberalism. *The New York Times*, November 18. Retrieved from https://www. nytimes.com/2016/11/20/opinion/sunday/the-end-of-identity-liberalism.html. Accessed on January 20, 2017.

MacWilliams, M. C. (2016). Who decides when the party doesn't? Authoritarian voters and the rise of Donald Trump. *PS: Political Science & Politics*, 49(4), 716−721.

Marantz, A. (2016). *Trolls for Trump: Meet Mike Cernovich, the meme mastermind of the alt-right*. October 31. Retrieved from http://www.newyorker.com/magazine/2016/10/31/trolls-for-trump. Accessed on January 23, 2017.

Markoe, L. (2016). *White Evangelicals, Catholics, and Mormons carried Trump*. November 9. Retrieved from religion news.com/2016/11/09/white-evangelicals-white-catholics-and-mormons-voted-decisively-for-trump/. Accessed on January 14, 2017.

Martin, J. (2016). Trump Institute offered get-rich schemes with plagiarized lessons. *The New York Times*, June 29. Retrieved from http://www.nytimes.com/2016/06/30/us/politics/donald-trump-institute-plagiarism.html?_r=0. Accessed on December 13, 2016.

Martin, J., & Burns, A. (2016). Blaming Muslims after attack, Donald Trump tosses pluralism aside. *The New York Times*, June 13. Retrieved from https://www.nytimes.com/2016/06/14/us/politics/donald-trump-hillary-clinton-speeches.html?_r=0. Accessed on April 28, 2017.

Marty, M. E. (1988). Fundamentalism as a social phenomenon. *Bulletin of the American Academy of Arts and Sciences*, 42(2), 15−29.

Mayer, J. (2016a). Donald Trump's ghost writer tells all. *The New Yorker*, July 25. Retrieved from http://www.newyorker.com/magazine/2016/07/25/donald-trumps-ghost-writer-tells-all. Accessed on August 24, 2016.

Mayer, J. (2016b). Donald Trump threatens the ghostwriter of 'the art of the deal'. *The New Yorker*, July 20. Retrieved from http://www.newyorker.com/news/news-desk/donald-trump-threatens-the-ghostwriter-of-the-art-of-the-deal Accessed on June 7, 2017.

Mayer, J. (2017). *Dark money: The hidden history of the billionaires behind the rise of the radical right*. New York, NY: Anchor.

Mazlish, B. (1973). *In search of Nixon: A psychohistorical inquiry*. New York, NY: Penguin.

McAdams, D. (2016). The mind of Donald Trump. *The Atlantic*, June. Retrieved from http://www.theatlantic.com/magazine/archive/2016/06/the-mind-of-donald-trump/480771/. Accessed on December 7, 2016.

Meagher, R. (2012). The 'vast right-wing conspiracy': Media and conservative networks. *New Political Science*, *34*(4), 469–484.

Mitchell, A., Gottfried, J., Barthel, M., & Shearer, E.. (2016). *Pathways to news*. Retrieved from http://www.journalism.org/2016/07/07/pathways-to-news/. Accessed on February 2, 2017.

Morin, R. (2014). *The demographics and politics of gun-owning households*. Pew Research Center, July 15. Retrieved from http://www.pewresearch.org/fact-tank/2014/07/15/the-demographics-and-politics-of-gun-owning-households/. Accessed on February 13, 2017.

Moyers, B. (2004). *Moyers on America: A journalist and his times*. New York, NY: Anchor Books.

Müller, J.-W. (2016). *What is populism?* Philadelphia, PA: University of Pennsylvania Press.

Obama, B. (2016). *Remarks by President Obama at Stavros Niarchos foundation cultural center in Athens*, Greece, November 16. Retrieved from https://obamawhitehouse. archives.gov/the-press-office/2016/11/16/remarks-president-obama-stavros-niarchos-foundation-cultural-center. Accessed on March 28, 2017.

O'Brien, T. L. (2005). *Trump nation: The art of being the Donald*. New York, NY: Warner Business Books.

Parker, K. (2016). Calm down. We'll be fine no matter who wins. *The Washington Post*, November 4. Retrieved from https://www.washingtonpost.com/opinions/calm-down-well-be-fine-no-matter-who-wins/2016/11/04/e5ca3c32-a2d3-11e6-a44d-cc2898cfab06_story.html?utm_term=. 97ced9f0b91c. Accessed on January 2, 2017.

Patterson, T. (2016). *News coverage of the 2016 general election: How the press failed the voters*: Harvard Kennedy School Shorenstein Center on Media, Politics, and Public Policy, December 7. Retrieved from https://shorensteincenter. org/news-coverage-2016-general-election/?platform=hoot-suite. Accessed on February 7, 2017.

Petrocelli, W. (2016). *Voters in Wyoming have 3.6 times the voting power that I have. It's time to end the Electoral College*. Retrieved from http://www.huffingtonpost.com/william-petrocelli/its-time-to-end-the-electoral-college_b_12891764.html. Accessed on December 30, 2016.

Pew Research Center. (2008). *False rumors that Obama is a Muslim*. November 20. Retrieved from http://www.journalism.org/2008/11/20/false-rumors-that-obama-is-a-muslim/. Accessed on December 16, 2016.

Pew Research Center. (2011). *The Tea Party and religion*. February 23. Retrieved from http://www.pewforum.org/2011/02/23/tea-party-and-religion/. Accessed on February 15, 2017.

Pew Research Center. (2012). *Nonvoters: Who they are, what they think*. November 1. Retrieved from http://www.people-press.org/2012/11/01/nonvoters-who-they-are-what-they-think/. Accessed on January 6, 2017.

Pew Research Center. (2014a). *Political polarization in the American Public*. June 12. Retrieved from http://www.people-press.org/2014/06/12/political-polarization-in-the-american-public/. Accessed on December 16, 2016.

Pew Research Center. (2014b). *Political polarization and media habits*. October 21. Retrieved from http://www.journalism.org/2014/10/21/political-polarization-media-habits/. Accessed on December 16, 2016.

Pew Research Center. (2015). *America's changing religious landscape*. May 12. Retrieved from http://www.pewforum.org/2015/05/12/americas-changing-religious-landscape/. Accessed on January 14, 2017.

Pew Research Center. (2016a). *A wider ideological gap between more and less educated adults*. April 26. Retrieved from http://www.people-press.org/2016/04/26/a-wider-ideological-gap-between-more-and-less-educated-adults/. Accessed on December 16, 2016.

Pew Research Center. (2016b). *Clinton, Trump supporters have starkly different views of a changing nation.* August 18. Retrieved from http://www.people-press.org/2016/08/18/clinton-trump-supporters-have-starkly-different-views-of-a-changing-nation/. Accessed on January 11, 2017.

Pew Research Center. (2017). *In first month, views of Trump are already strongly felt, deeply polarized.* February 16. Retrieved from http://www.people-press.org/2017/02/16/in-first-month-views-of-trump-are-already-strongly-felt-deeply-polarized/. Accessed on April 5, 2017.

Phillips, K. P. (1970). *The emerging republican majority.* Garden City, NY: Anchor Books.

Postman, N. (1985). *Amusing ourselves to death: Public discourse in the age of show business.* New York, NY: Viking.

Prior, M. (2013). Media and political polarization. *Annual Review of Political Science, 16,* 101–127.

PRRI. (2013). *New survey finds increased support for better mental health services to prevent future mass shootings, stricter gun control laws.* January 23. Retrieved from http://www.prri.org/press-release/january-2013-rtp-release-1/. Accessed on February 14, 2017.

Purdum, T. S. (2014a). *An idea whose time has come: Two presidents, two parties, and the battle for the Civil Rights Act of 1964.* New York, NY: Henry Holt and Co.

Purdum, T. S. (2014b). Why the civil rights couldn't pass today. *Politico,* July 2. Retrieved from http://www.politico.com/story/2014/07/why-the-civil-rights-act-couldnt-pass-today-108496. Accessed on February 8, 2017.

Quinnipiac University Poll. (2017). *Trump slump continues as he drops below Obama, Quinnipiac University National*

Poll finds; Republicans in Congress drop to more than 3-1 negative. April 4. Retrieved from https://poll.qu.edu/images/polling/us/us04042017_U423fmbh.pdf/. Accessed on April 5, 2017.

Regan, M. 2016. What does voter turnout tell us about the 2016 election? *PBS Newshour*, November 20. Retrieved from http://www.pbs.org/newshour/updates/voter-turnout-2016-elections/. Accessed on January 9, 2016.

Reich, R. (2016). Trump: The American fascist. *Moyers & Company*, March 11. Retrieved from http://billmoyers.com/story/trump-the-american-fascist/. Accessed on December 15, 2016.

Riesebrodt, M. (1993). In D. Reneau (Trans.). *Pious passion: The emergence of modern fundamentalism in the United States and Iran*, Berkeley, CA: University of California Press.

Robinson, E. (2016). Is Donald Trump just plain crazy? *The Washington Post*, August 1. Retrieved from https://www.washingtonpost.com/opinions/is-donald-trump-just-plain-crazy/2016/08/01/. Accessed on December 4, 2016.

Robinson, M. (2015). *The givenness of things: Essays.* New York, NY: Farrar, Straus and Giroux.

Rosenthal, M. J. (2016). How Trump went bust and got rich using other people's money: A timeline. *Mother Jones*, October 14. Retrieved from http://www.motherjones.com/politics/2016/10/how-donald-trump-destroyed-his-empire-and-dumped-ruins-others-timeline.

Ross, A. (2016). The Frankfurt school knew Trump was coming. *The New Yorker*, December 5. Retrieved from http://www.newyorker.com/culture/cultural-comment/the-

frankfurt-school-knew-trump-was-coming. Accessed on
December 22, 2016.

Roth, P. (2004). *The plot against America*. New York, NY:
Houghton Mifflin.

Schlesinger, A., Jr. (1949). *The vital center: The politics of
freedom*. Boston, MA: Houghton Mifflin Company.

Schmitt, C. (1996 [1932]). *The concept of the political*, translated and introduced by George Schwab. Chicago, IL:
University of Chicago Press.

Schudson, M. (2008). *Why democracies need an unlovable
press*. Cambridge: Polity Press.

Seipel, A. (2016). *Trump makes unfounded claim that
'Millions' voted illegally for Clinton*. National Public Radio,
November 27. Retrieved from http://www.npr.org/2016/11/
27/503506026/trump-makes-unfounded-claim-that-millions-
voted-illegally-for-clinton. Accessed on December 30, 2016.

Sherman, G. (2014). *The loudest voice in the room:
How the brilliant, bombastic Roger Ailes built Fox
News—and divided a country*. New York, NY: Random
House.

Shils, E. (1991). The virtue of civil society. *Government and
Opposition*, 26(1), 3–20.

Shklar, J. N. (1990). *The faces of injustice*. New Haven, CT:
Yale University Press.

Silver, N. (2016a). *Education, not income, predicted who
would vote for Trump*. November 22. Retrieved from http://
fivethirtyeight.com/features/education-not-income-predicted-
who-would-vote-for-trump/. Accessed on December 16,
2016.

Silver, N. (2016b). *The mythology of Trump's 'Working Class' support*. May 3. Retrieved from http://fivethirtyeight.com/features/education-not-income-predicted-who-would-vote-for-trump/. Accessed on November 8, 2016.

Singer, M. (1997). Trump solo. *The New Yorker*, May 19. Retrieved from http://www.thenewyorker.com/magazine/1997/05/19/trump-solo/. Accessed on December 8, 2016.

Skocpol, T. (2013). Why the Tea Party isn't going anywhere. *The Atlantic*, December 26. Retrieved from https://www.theatlantic.com/politics/archive/2013/12/why-the-tea-party-isnt-going-anywhere/282591/. Accessed on February 15, 2017.

Skocpol, T., & Williamson, V. (2012). *The Tea Party and the remaking of Republican conservatism*. New York, NY: Oxford University Press.

Smith, C. (1998). *American Evangelicalism: Embattled and thriving*. Chicago, IL: University of Chicago Press.

Somers, M. (2001). Romancing the market, reviling the state: Historicizing liberalization, privatization, and the compelling claims to civil society. In C. Crouch, K. Eder, & D. Tambini (Eds.), *Citizenship, markets, and the state* (pp. 23–48). New York, NY: Oxford University Press.

Stanley, J. (2016). *How propaganda works*. Princeton, NJ: Princeton University Press.

Stenner, K. (2005). *The authoritarian dynamic*. New York, NY: Cambridge University Press.

Stuart, T. (2016). Donald Trump's thirteen biggest business failures. *Rolling Stone*, March 14. Retrieved from http://www.rollingstone.com/politics/news/donald-trumps-13-

biggest-business-failures-20160314. Accessed on December 13, 2016.

Sykes, C. J. (2017). The Right that Cried Wolf. *The New York Times*, February 5, pp. R1, R4.

The Economist. (2016). Deconstructing Donald. *The Economist*, November 26, pp. 59–60.

The Economist Intelligence Unit. (2017). *Democracy index 2016: Revenge of the "Deplorables"*. Retrieved from http:// www.eiu.com/public/topical_report.aspx?campaignid= DemocracyIndex2016. Accessed on January 31, 2017.

Trump, D. (2015). Letter to the editor. *New York Times*, September 11. Retrieved from http://www.nytimes.com/2005/ 09/11/opinion/character-studies-815985.html?_r=0. Accessed on June 7, 2017.

U.S. Bureau of the Census. (2016). *Quick facts: United States*. Retrieved from https://www.census.gov/quickfacts/ table/PST045216/00. Accessed on January 6, 2017.

Uggen, C., Larson, R., & Shannon, S. (2016). *6 million lost voters: State-level estimates of felony disenfranchisement, 2016*. Washington, DC: The Sentencing Project.

Waldman, M. (2014). The rise of the NRA. *Moyers & Company*. June 12. Retrieved from http://billmoyers.com/ 2014/06/12/the-rise-of-the-nra-2/. Accessed on February 13, 2017.

Wallace, T., & Parlapiano, A. (2017). Crowd scientists say women's march had 3 times as many people as Trump's inauguration. *The New York Times*, January 22. Retrieved from https://www.nytimes.com/interactive/2017/01/22/us/politics/ womens-march-trump-crowd-estimates.html?_r=0. Accessed on April 5, 2017.

Wasserman, D. (2017). 2016 popular vote tracker. *The Cook Political Report*, January 3, 2017. Retrieved from http://cookpolitical.com/story/10174. Accessed on January 6, 2017.

Weiler, J. (2016). *Demystifying the Trump coalition: It's the authoritarianism*. September 4. Retrieved from http://www.huffingtonpost.com/jonathan-weiler/demystifying-the-trump-co_b_8089380.html. Accessed on January 13, 2017.

Wemple, E. (2016). Study: Clinton-Trump coverage was a feast of false equivalency. *The Washington Post*, December 7. Retrieved from https://www.washingtonpost.com/blogs/erik-wemple/wp/2016/12/07/study-clinton-trump-coverage-was-a-feast-of-false-equivalency/?utm_term=.ad9f0b1940f5. Accessed on February 7, 2017.

Williams, R. (2009). Politicized Evangelicalism and secular elites: Creating a moral other. In S. Brint & J. R. Schroedel (Eds.), *Evangelicals and democracy in America, Vol. II: Religion and politics* (pp. 143–178). New York, NY: Russell Sage Foundation.

Yanker, J. (2014). *'From My Cold Dead Hands': The role of the NRA in the lack of gun reform in the United States from 1996—2014*. Boulder, CO: University of Colorado, CU Scholar.

Zylstra, S. E. (2016). Dobson explains why he called trump a baby Christian. *Christianity Today*, August 4. Retrieved from http://www.christianitytoday.com/gleanings/2016/august/james-dobson-explains-why-donald-trump-baby-christian.html. Accessed on February 14, 2017.

INDEX

Printed in the USA
CPSIA information can be obtained
at www.ICGtesting.com
JSHW062028300823
47577JS00012B/227

9 781787 143685